ANGKOR

CITIES AND TEMPLES

ANGKOR
CITIES AND TEMPLES

Claude Jacques
Photographs Michael Freeman

Translation Tom White

RIVER BOOKS

First edition published in Thailand in 1997 by
River Books Co., Ltd.
396 Maharaj Road, Tatien, Bangkok 10200
Tel. 66 2 6221900, 2254963, 2246686 Fax. 66 2 2253861
E-mail: riverps@ksc.th.com
www.riverbooksbk.com
Reprinted 2000, 2003 & 2005

British Library Cataloguing-in-Publication Data.
A catalogue record for this book is available from the British Library.

ISBN: 974 8225 15 1

Editor and Publisher Narisa Chakrabongse
Design Supadee Ruangsakvichit
Production Supervision Paisarn Piemmettawat

Colour separation by Sirivatana Interprint Public Co., Ltd.
Printed and bound in Thailand by Sirivatana Interprint Public Co., Ltd.

Previous pages: Angkor Wat from Phnom Bakheng.
Pages 6-7: Bakong at sunrise.

CONTENTS

FOREWORD

There are excellent reasons for Claude Jacques to have written this new book on Angkor. Following the 'solemn appeal' which I made in November 1991, and the 'Tokyo Declaration' of October 1993, a co-ordinated internation effort has been set up to safeguard and develop Angkor. Despite the huge challenge, the formidable obstacles and the many perils, all concerned have regained their confidence and hope. Four years of determined effort have been rewarded with remarkable success.

In a way, history has been 'extended', and no longer comes to a halt at the beginning of the thirteenth century. After Angkor Thom ('the great capital'), Angkor Wat ('the capital which became a temple') remained active until at least the middle of the fifteenth century. This means that the Khmer empire enjoyed almost seven centuries of prosperity.

Further research in Khmer architecture has given new insights into the originality and coherence of these ancient temples, each of which is a unique creation while remaining firmly attached to Indian tradition. The research has also highlighted the achievements of the hydraulic engineers and the skill of the geometricians.

The high quality of Khmer artistic achievement has also become more and more evident, with the great exhibition of sculpture shown in Paris, Washington and Tokyo in 1997 and 1998. The talents of the Khmer sculptors, both in the round and in the remarkable relief carvings, reflect their ceaseless desire for innovation and their abundant imagination.

In this book the reader will find the latest discoveries about Angkor, thanks to its luminous text and its spellbinding photographs. In the first light of day, the shrines can look like giants clothed in greenery, whilst at sunset, the stones stand out against the vegetation. It is another miracle of Angkor: 40,000 hectares of natural and stone forest entwined with each other. I see this not as confrontation but as harmony: a mutual celebration of vital impulse and creativity. Seeing is believing . . .but the lessons of Angkor can help broaden everyone's view.

Federico Mayor
Director General, UNESCO
Paris, 1997

Opposite: The Northern entrance, Ta Prohm.

PREFACE

The first edition of this book was published in French only by Editions Bordas in France in 1990. The text of this edition has been thoroughly revised and updated to take into account the new discoveries and theories which have appeared since then, and the illustrations are almost completely new. Essentially this is a new book and is the first of my books to be available in English, having been admirably translated by Tom White who spent several years in Phnom Penh.

Despite certain setbacks, Cambodia has made a courageous recovery from the cataclysm of the 1970s, although much indeed remains to be done. The 'park' of Angkor has been reopened for research and for tourist access. From 1986 to 1992, India had already made a significant contribution towards its rehabilitation, whilst the International Co-ordination Committee to safeguard the monuments of Angkor, under the joint presidency of France and Japan, thanks to the invaluable support of UNESCO which provides its secretariat, has spared no effort in setting up projects for research, restoration and site clearance, with teams and support from America, France, Germany, Hungary, Indonesia, Italy, Japan and Luxemburg.

Since the West discovered this marvellous complex of monuments there has been a considerable volume of research, mainly carried out by the French scholars of the Ecole française d'Extrême-Orient. Prominent among these was George Cœdès, who with other experts sketched the first outlines of the history of ancient Cambodia on the basis of their reading of the epigraphs. The whole story of the political and social life of the ancient Khmers is however still far from being fully known or understood.

Nevertheless, the reopening of Angkor affords new opportunities for the research community to test the more or less fanciful theories which have been propounded, inevitably from afar, during the too many 'dark years' which Cambodia has had to endure. This book presents a provisional account of ongoing research, and attempts to give a clearer picture of the facts than was possible at the time when our predecessors were conducting their invaluable pioneering investigations. I would like to thank René Dumont for his contribution to the sculpture section and Tom White for his sensitive translation.

It is to the undying memory of George Cœdès, who kindly requested that I should pursue his research, that I dedicate this book.

Claude Jacques
Paris, 1997

Opposite: Detail from a battle scene, Bayon.

11

A New Map of EAST INDIA.

Sold by Tho: Basset in Fleetstreet.
and Richard Chiswell in St. Pauls
Church yard.

Chapter one

KHMER CIVILISATION

At its height the Khmer civilisation, centred on Angkor, extended as far west as the present day border of Thailand and Burma and north as far as Wat Phu in Laos. Even the central area alone covered an area of some 400 square kilometres, and today's visitor can discover several centuries of history jumbled together, from the eighth century Prasat Ak Yum to the fourteenth century Mangalartha, and even as far as the sixteenth century when there were attempts by a Khmer king to 'restore' Angkor Wat.

Angkor, which means 'capital city', is one of the Khmer language terms for the Sanskrit *nagara* which means 'town'. It retains its meaning in the derivation of several toponyms in modern Cambodia, such as Angkor Borei, south of Phnom Penh. In the region of Siem Reap, north-east of the Great Lake, it is particularly used to name the groups of Angkor Wat ('the town which is a temple') and Angkor Thom ('the great town').

From the end of the ninth century in what is now called 'Angkor Archaeological Park' there was a succession of capitals (at least seven have been identified) on sites sometimes quite distant from each other. The old Khmer title for these was generally the same: Yasodharapura, 'the town of him who bears glory', taken from the name of Angkor's first founder, Yasovarman I. There were thus considerable changes over this period, modifying the environment as various projects were undertaken, many of them of gigantic proportions, but many also of short duration. The capital would only attain stability at the end of the twelfth century, when for the first time in the region's history, the great king Jayavarman VII decided to enclose it in walls of such girth that his successors decided to remain there whatever the cost. The building of new religious monuments continued within this enclosure at least until 1431 AD, which is the traditional (and probably inaccurate) date of what has been called 'the abandonment of Angkor'.

Stone Ganesha early 10th century. (Ubon National Museum, Thailand)

Opposite: 17th century map of South-East Asia.

13

The shrine of a local deity. (Photo: Claude Jacques)

Right: Bas-relief from the Bayon, showing a woman selling fish from under a typical wooden pavilion.

Opposite: 1902 map by Lunet de Lajonquière showing the density of temples (in red) to the north of Angkor.

The history which we believe we can glimpse nowadays is a history that the Khmers had long forgotten. It has had to be pieced together from fragmentary evidence which has left many shadowy gaps, through the work of researchers, in the main from France, who from the late nineteenth century have studied the temples of the Khmer country and the inscriptions carved in stone which have been found in or near them. Almost nothing remains of domestic dwellings, even those of the kings, except for a few scattered tiles discovered more or less accidentally. The Khmers lived in wooden houses which have long since disappeared, although in 1996 during excavations at the royal palace of Angkor Thom sockets of wooden pillars were discovered. These are in an excellent state of preservation and seem to date from the end of the ninth or the early tenth century. Similar discoveries are, however, bound to be few and far between, and the fact of the matter is that the rediscovery of the life and history of the Khmers has had to be based mainly on a study of the evidence provided by their religious activities.

It is true that some other sources of information which might be thought more objective are also available. The most notable of these are the Chinese Dynastic Annals, to which should be added the account of his visit to Angkor written by the 'ambassador' Zhou Daguan at the end of the thirteenth century. The Chinese indeed took an interest from very early times in the peoples of surrounding countries, not so much in order to conquer them but to set up trading links. For this reason, the Dynastic Annals make frequent references to them, and scholars have generally given these much credence on the grounds that, according to them, they contain much more truthful and concrete information than can be gleaned from the indigenous sources themselves. We will seek to modify this over-subscribed view.

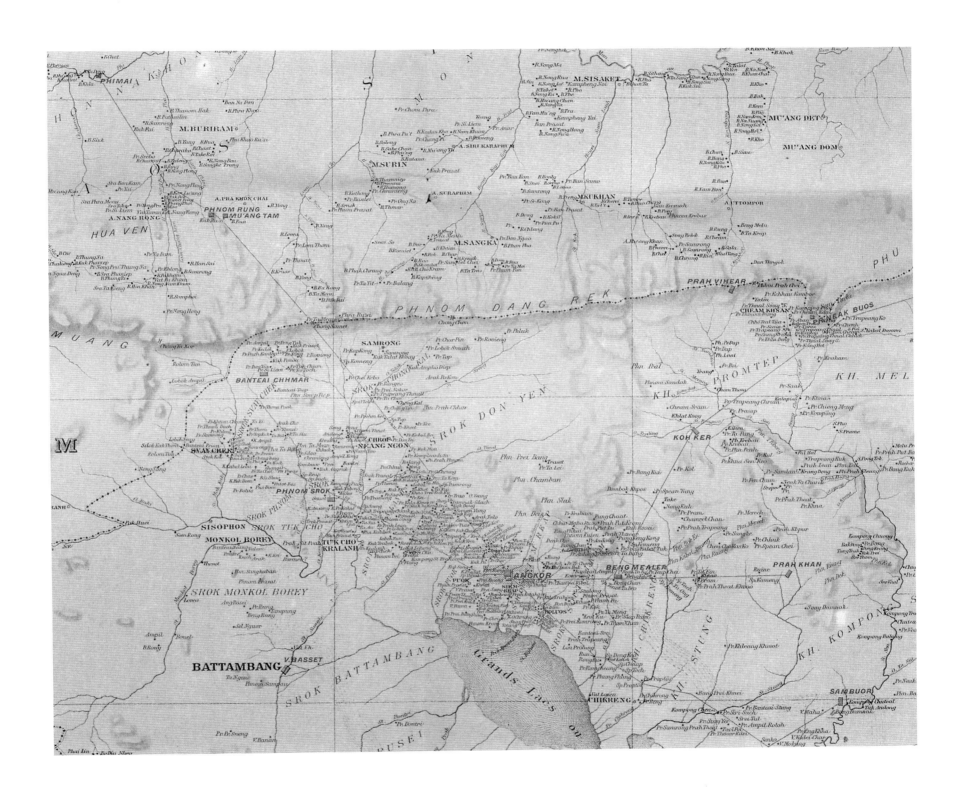

THE INSCRIPTIONS

The most ancient indigenous writings to have been found are carved in stone, the only medium which could, to an extent, withstand the ravages of time. They date from the fifth and sixth centuries, and are in Sanskrit. Not long after, in a text dated 612 AD, there appears the Khmer language, but already with many loan-words from Sanskrit, perhaps because all the stone inscriptions are closely concerned with Hindu or Buddhist religious practice. Sanskrit indeed came with Indian travellers, whose gods were adopted by the Khmers, and perhaps first of all by their kings. They thus needed to use the indispensable language in which their prayers and worship were expressed. Some 1,200 inscriptions in Sanskrit and Khmer have been found in the land formerly occupied by the Khmers, most of which have been translated and published by George Cœdès, the doyen of Khmer studies. They were carved from the sixth to the fourteenth centuries, and generally placed in shrines. They are exclusively religious documents, by which I mean that they always concern religion or the administration of the temples. Of course, here and there, there are allusions to the life of the 'laity' which give precious hints about the everyday life of the Khmers, but these are never the main aim of a text. The inscriptions are the principal sources from which, in one way or another, the ancient history of the Khmer country can be retraced. Truth to tell, given the reasons for their existence, it is almost miraculous that they reveal so much about this history. In contrast, the inscriptions of neighbouring peoples such as the Mons of Thailand, for example, are infinitely poorer in historical data.

It is important to understand clearly why the ancient Khmers took so much trouble to engrave texts in Sanskrit, in Khmer, or in both languages, in stone, sometimes with such skill that the stones are real works of art. Sanskrit was the learned language of India, and probably always remained little-used by the population outside the temples, but it was quite simply the language of the Hindu gods whom they worshipped and for whom they contrived to build their remarkable temples. The gods brought them prosperity in this world and beatitude in the next, so they had to be well looked after on the one hand, and well understood on the other, through the medium of the only language they could understand.

With very few exceptions, Sanskrit exists as poetic texts in more or less elaborate language according to the capacity of the author. These works were addressed to a particular god and were apparently meant to attract his attention to a man who had honoured him by building a shrine, or more often by offering gifts. In most cases the poem seems to have been composed on the death of the donor, at the critical moment when he had most need of the god he had served.

Detail of the inscription opposite, from face D at the beginning of stanza 149 to 157. It lists the various materials used in the temple construction – tin, plumb, iron, stones, pearls. It also lists the number of towers – 414, and length of walls – 16,000 spans.

Opposite: The foundation stele, K 908, from Preah Khan which bears the date 1191. It is now housed in the Angkor Conservancy.

Sanskrit inscription on stele K 528 from the East Mebon. It is dated January 958 and comprises a long poem eulogising King Rajendravarman.

The shape of these poems is almost always identical. After one or several verses which salute the temple god and those around him, there is the 'genealogy' of the benefactor, which in practice contains only the names of those of his ancestors who enjoyed some sort of fame. Next comes the eulogy of the benefactor himself, occasionally including interesting biographical facts, followed by an account of other donations he has made, and then of course the specific foundation which is the object of the inscription, and the date (where applicable) on which it was dedicated to the god. The poet finally invokes blessings on the foundation's future guardians, and curses, in one or several verses, on the wretches who might seek to destroy it.

Both the length and the quality of these poems show considerable variation, but it is exceptional to come across one which is really mediocre. Some can be very long. The Pre Rup stele is the longest and probably the finest and is a poem of almost 300 verses, the equivalent of 1000 of our alexandrines. They are usually written in a specifically Indian poetic style, *kavya*, which draws extensively on metaphors mainly from Hindu mythology or from Indian epics, thus emphasising their authors' breadth of culture.

The founder could be a king, but there were often temples built by dignitaries or families. These substantial pious works implied great wealth and their patrons were therefore close to the throne. They rarely fail to mention the names of the kings they served, together with short eulogies which are an asset to historians since this sometimes allows them to make fruitful chronological comparisons.

To be sure, these documents are by no means objective. It is certain that they contain nothing unfavourable to the dedicatee and, paradoxically, little which is derogatory to his enemies, especially if they are kings. It should be noted that the latter, once consecrated and especially once cremated, were imbued with potentially dangerous power, and it was thus prudent to propitiate them.

The Khmer language texts on the other hand are of quite a different type. In the overwhelming majority of cases they are in the form of inventories, listing temple goods, lands, cattle, minor servants, movable objects, etc. The lists should not however be considered exhaustive, as they generally refer to donations by a specific individual, often the founder praised in the Sanskrit poem when the inscription is bilingual. They nevertheless provide information on the ancient economy, although little research on this aspect has been undertaken to date.

These are not mere lists. To take the example of paddy fields, there are frequent references to their price and to the names of their former owners, and occasionally we are given details of the litigation they have given rise to. These are the most interesting texts as they lift the curtain on certain aspects of 'secular' life. In exceptional cases, as the inscription recounts the history of a temple's wealth, it can give a glimpse of one or several centuries of history, as it refers to the kings who were ministered to by the line of descendants of the temple's owners. There are cases in which different temples are co-owners of paddy fields, and others where one or several minor temples declare their 'co-participation' in a grander one. This resulted in the payment of dues by the smaller ones to the larger, with the former benefiting in exchange from the protection and prestige of the latter.

There are interminable lists of servants of both sexes (most often referred to as 'slaves') which are typically found in the royal temples of the ninth and tenth centuries. These people worked either in the temple or in the paddy fields. They cannot have been real slaves for the simple reason that slaves were strictly forbidden from entering a temple, where their presence would have defiled it. It is therefore scarcely imaginable that their names were so carefully carved beneath the very eyes of the gods.

Other lists concern temple furniture, particularly the jewellery with which the gods were adorned, and other essential ritual objects. These are of particular value as the objects themselves have vanished completely.

In general, certain trends in the composition of these inscriptions can be observed. Thus the best quality Sanskrit poems appear at the end of the ninth century and the middle of the tenth, and during these periods the long lists of 'slaves' also occur. In contrast there is a particular abundance of royal decrees concerning the temples towards the end of the tenth century, whereas in the eleventh there are often

Khmer inscription K 73 found at Wat Phra That near Phnom Penh, 7th century.

Left: Part of the 9th century inscription from the door frame of Phnom Wan in north-east Thailand.

Bas-relief of woman about to give birth under a small pavilion, southern outer gallery, Bayon.

Above: Prisoners, eastern outer gallery, Bayon.

histories of temples belonging to specific lineages, and these are a precious source for the historian. Furthermore, the short inscriptions recording the name of the god residing in such and such a shrine hardly ever occur before the twelfth century. These trends have to be reckoned with, and it is eminently possible that a custom recorded in the inscriptions of a given period could also have been observed in other times without it being felt necessary to record it.

KHMER LITERATURE

Khmer civilisation created many admirable visual works of art and all the evidence is that it also produced an abundance of literature in a wide variety of genres, as the inscriptions bear witness. But nothing remains of the contents of the manuscripts, as the climate and the insects ensured that they would never survive for long. It is perplexing, therefore, that there appear to have been no scribes to copy out the manuscripts which crammed the libraries.

We do have an idea, however, of what these libraries might have contained. The Chinese traveller Zhou Daguan at the end of the thirteenth century mentions "writings in chalk on blackened skins" and there were certainly also palm-leaf manuscripts, written on latania leaves, a practice which is widespread to this day. The inscriptions swarm with references to classical Indian literature, the great epics of the *Mahabharata* and the *Ramayana,* texts on ritual and grammar, and on the *Dharmasastra,* which are treatises on the Law regulating the order of the world. Similarly, the extensive reliefs and carvings are prolific with scenes from the Indian epics. The horoscopes show a good knowledge of astronomy, and, in sum, the men of letters bear witness to a vast culture of Indian origin.

It is hard to imagine that at the same time there was not also a substantial body of original Khmer literature, although it scarcely figures in the inscriptions. It has nevertheless left some vestiges. Two Khmer language inscriptions allow us to discover three authentic extracts from 'royal chronicles' which are analogous to the ones we know today. The first concerns the miraculous origin of a temple in the reign of Jayavarman III in the mid-ninth century. The other two both describe why two noble warriors of the second half of the twelfth century were honoured in the temple of Banteay Chhmar, after their heroic deaths.

It is known, moreover, that these 'annals' were regularly updated and conserved, as they have been until recent times, by officials of the royal household. The epigraphic record reveals that at the beginning of these works, as is the case today, there were chapters of an entirely legendary nature. What a boon it would be to have access to such texts, whether legendary or historical!

KHMER SOCIETY

The most difficult task is to glimpse in the written record the lives of the Khmer people, and it is only in the reliefs of Bayon temple at the end of the twelfth century that we can see them to some extent in their day to day existence. Even then, the few scenes depicted are quite insufficient to allow us to understand the social structure of the country. The size of the monuments has led some to seek to make comparisons with other civilisations such as ancient Egypt; in fact, far removed from the Khmers in time and space. Using the *Devaraja* myth (the God-King), historians have gone on to imagine a theocratic society composed of a tiny minority of priests obeying an all-powerful king, and ruling over a population of slaves.

The reality was indubitably quite different. It is true that today we can only understand this civilisation in its religious aspects, and that there are few reliable elements to allow an appreciation of everyday life. But we should not allow ourselves to be overwhelmed by the religious evidence to the point where we cannot imagine what the reality of life outside the temples might have been like. In order to do this our best guide might well be the lives of the Khmer people in the nineteenth century as described, for example, by Adhemard Leclere who was the French Resident in the North-East of Cambodia and a perfect observer of Khmer society and customs.

On the basis that only the paddy fields described in the inscriptions are the ones for which we have formal evidence, it has too often been maintained that the temples were practically the only landowners in the country in ancient times. Common sense indicates to the contrary that there were also private owners of paddy fields, even if these were only those who on occasion donated them to the temples.

These great landowners, along with certain major temples which could well have been in possession of vast areas of paddy fields, are clearly mentioned in the texts of the late twelfth century. But it would be unwise to go no further, and conclude that ancient Khmer society did not have smallholders. In fact there is no proof that it was fundamentally different from what has been described in more recent times, and we might not be too far from the truth if we imagine a land which was mostly divided among the peasant majority.

What is evident from the inscriptions is that society was highly structured in so far as a man's name is generally preceded by a title or appellation which designated his rank. The meanings of these terms, and the relative hierarchical positions they denote, are mostly unknown to us. Nevertheless, the structure was relatively flexible, as titles were bestowed by the king, who could consequently replace them with others, and they were not automatically hereditary.

The 'kings of kings' could even elevate others to be kings, conferring the title on a personal and quasi-'honorary' basis. At least two examples are known of high

Decapitated heads, being held aloft, southern outer gallery, Banteay Chhmar.

Above: A prince and courtiers, southern outer gallery, Bayon.

Ceramic-making, southern outer gallery, Bayon.

dignitaries, both of them tutors and counsellors of the king, being given such a title in the mid-eleventh century. Udayadityavarman II conferred the royal name of Jayendravarman on his guru Sadasiva, and at the end of the twelfth century Jayavarman VII made a similar grant to his own guru, giving him the name Jayamangalarthadeva, and adding that his family members would have the right to the title 'king's relative'. A trace of this practice can still be seen when Prince Norodom Sihanouk, as he was formerly called, and King Sihanoukvarman, as he is now, conferred and still confers in exceptional cases the royal title of *Samdech* on Khmer high dignitaries.

The inscriptions provide us with still more titles of office in the royal court, in the judiciary and even in local administration. In so far as we do not always know their place in the hierarchy, it is difficult to draw up a coherent table to allow us to understand these administrative structures.

Additionally there were the priests, who sometimes claimed to be 'Brahmins'. It is indeed only for them that the notion of 'caste', sometimes alluded to by the Indian term *varna*, could have had a meaning in so far as their positions seem to have been hereditary. Some of these priests appear to have been classified in a sort of caste system with a nomenclature which is occasionally referred to, but the details of the system remain obscure. We know that King Jayavarman V instituted two of these Brahmin castes and personally chose the members who were to belong to them. For his part, Suryavarman I, following the upheavals which his accession to the throne had provoked, was quick to confirm some Brahmins in their caste, whilst others were pitilessly expelled.

As concerns ordinary people, all we have are the lists of 'slaves' which have already been mentioned and which will be discussed later. If it is the case, as I think it is, that these people were actually only the slaves of their god, the documentary evidence suggests after all a Khmer society of farmers who were closely linked to the life of their temple, as they have been in recent times, and are indeed now. Once more, we can imagine how things were by observing the way they are now.

There were, however, real slaves, although here again distinctions must be made. On the one hand there were believers who 'gave' slaves to certain temples, always in small numbers and identified by name. These could have been 'debt-slaves', or even poor people for whom a believer gave a sort of rent to a temple in exchange for their subsistence. In these cases their regime must not have been too strict. On the other hand there were captives and people who came from displaced neighbouring populations, especially those who lived in distant mountainous regions and were considered as savages. These were sometimes enumerated in the inscriptions, but never mentioned by name, and it is likely that their fate was anything but enviable.

THE LINEAGES

The lines of descent were matrilineal, so continuity passed through the female line, although generally inscriptions only record the names of men. They were of considerable importance which shows up in various ways, notably through the ownership of temples managed by a warden chosen from among themselves. As well as the Hindu gods, these temples doubtless also housed the ancestral guardians who in time of need provided counsel to their descendants through the voice of a medium, as was the standard practice until recent times.

The most eminent lineage, which naturally soon split into innumerable sub-lineages, would have consisted of the kings, the descendants of the founder-kings: Kaundinya and his spouse Soma, on one hand, and Kambu and Mera, on the other. These four personages seem to be completely mythical and they in fact spring from two separate legends. We can see that all the Khmer kings claimed descent from one couple or the other, as if such a claim was an indispensable adjunct to the right to the throne. It should be noted that there was nothing resembling our primogeniture in determining the succession of Khmer kings, who were simply chosen from within the royal family, unless – as was most frequently the case – they seized power by force. A quick glance at the succession of 'the kings of kings' reveals that it usually took place in anarchic and even violent circumstances.

Rice baskets, southern outer gallery Bayon.

Left: A boar fight, southern outer gallery Bayon.

Ladies-in-waiting, south-east corner pavilion, Bayon.

Opposite: King Suryavarman II seated on his throne from the reliefs on the southern gallery of bas-reliefs, Angkor Wat.

THE KING AND THE ROYAL DYNASTIES

Formerly, and indeed in recent times, the two essential moments in a reign were the consecration of the king, making him the supreme protector of the people of whom he was the incarnation, thereby becoming a sacred person, and his cremation, whereby he was incorporated for evermore among the numerous guardian divinities of his kingdom. The first of these two ceremonies could take place several months or even more after the de facto assumption of power, since it was particularly important to await the favourable astrological moment. It apparently took place according to a solemn ritual well known in India, which lasted several days. Whilst all kings were crowned in this way, the supreme 'kings of Khmer kings' were consecrated in another ceremony, of which the grandeur can be imagined.

It was at this point that they received their 'regnal names' which were distinguished, following Indian precedent, by the final syllables *varman* meaning 'breast-plate' or 'protection'. So Jayavarman means 'he who has victory as his breast-plate', or 'he who is protected by victory'. It is evident that the original meaning was soon forgotten and the suffix merely indicated that its bearer had been crowned king.

The solemn cremation of a king also doubtless followed a ritual derived from India, but at least as concerned the 'kings of kings', specifically Khmer elements were added. The defunct king received a posthumous name which indicated precisely into which world he had passed, so Yashovarman 1 became 'the king who departed into the world of the supreme Shiva', Paramashivaloka. The name was unambiguously the king's after his death, since in contrast to the regnal name, it was given on an individual basis. For some unknown reason it is almost exclusively used in the Khmer texts, whilst the Sanskrit poems carry on citing the regnal name.

George Cœdès, in writing Khmer history, quite naturally concentrated on tracing the royal dynasties, and in his zealous pursuit of the lineages of 'legitimate' kings he did not take into account that these were very often in fact interrupted, not so much by the lack of an inheritor to those who held power as by the claimant of a different branch of the line who seized the throne with a greater or lesser degree of brute force. It is quite evident that of the twenty-six supreme kings recorded in the period of Angkor, only eight were sons or brothers of the preceding king. Moreover, even among these eight, at least two seized the throne against the advice of their fathers, one of them being no less a figure than Yashovarman I, the founder of the first city of Angkor. It can thus be seen that in the succession to Angkor, the accepted idea of 'legitimacy' was not one which enjoyed the special respect of the claimants, and 'usurpation' was more or less the rule.

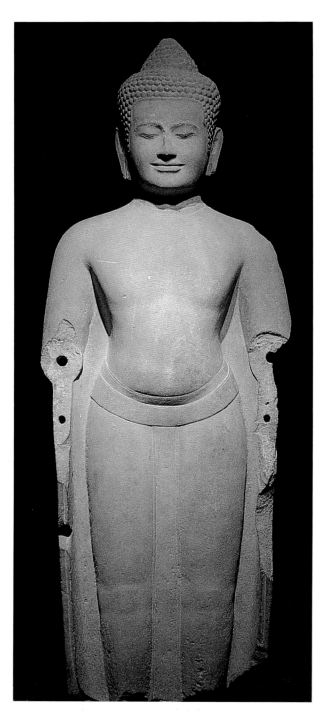

It has perhaps been a mistake to look for 'rules of succession' where none had really been established. It should not be forgotten that Jayavarman II, after conquering a number of Khmer kingdoms, founded an empire by having a special ceremony to confer on himself the title of *chakravartin*, or 'world emperor'. He certainly wished that the empire he had thus constituted should survive him, and to ensure this he not only had himself crowned but also instituted his counterpart in the divine realm: the famous *Devaraja*. There were undoubtedly rules of succession for the traditional Khmer kings, who were rulers of their own kingdoms, but there appears to have been no reason why these same kings could have quietly agreed that a sole lineage should become their eternal overlord on the supreme throne. It may be the origin of the 'disorder' of which we have proof, and is sad for historians.

THE RELIGIONS

Why was it so easy for the indigenous people to adopt the gods the Indians had brought with them to South-East Asia? It may perhaps be imagined that the success of the Indians with their novel methods was ascribed to divine protection, and that the Khmers and the Chams accordingly began to establish them in their temples. Moreover these foreign gods could readily find a place beside the local deities, as they had already done in India, within what was doubtless a very similar cosmology. Thus particular devotion was accorded to the gods Shiva and Vishnu, and also to the Buddha. Shiva, however, is the dominant figure, as he was long considered by the kings as supreme protector of their empire. It is thus to him that most of the temples are dedicated, and he in turn had to ensure the prosperity of the kingdom.

The proliferation of sects which flourished in India does not feature in the land of the Khmers, however. As in other domains, the Khmers were the assiduous pupils of their first teachers, and do not seem to have sought to delve deeper into doctrines which perhaps remained somewhat alien to them, nor indeed to dispute them by proposing new ones. It is for this reason that only one or two sects of each of the Shivaite or Vishnuite 'religions' are known. Similarly it is probable that Buddhism, of which much less is known, was not broken down into numerous sects, although besides Mahayana Buddhism, the so-called Greater vehicle, which was more widespread, there is some early evidence for the existence of followers of Theravada Buddhism.

The temples as seen today give only a sketchy idea of the total number of shrines which adorned the land of the Khmers. Despite being built in durable materials, implying considerable wealth on the part of their builders, many must have disappeared over the centuries. Furthermore, they were far from being the only Hindu

Standing Buddha, Bayon style. (Musée Guimet)

Heads of the three principal Hindu gods from Phnom Bok. In the Bakheng style, they date to c. 900 AD. (Musée Guimet)

Top: Brahma
Left: Shiva
Above: Vishnu

11th century carving showing Shiva and his consort, Uma, riding on the bull Nandi. Lintel on the northern tower of Muang Tam in north-east Thailand.

shrines in the Khmer country, as others were built by the less wealthy in perishable materials. The inscriptions reveal that sometimes there were years of delay before being able to build a shrine of durable materials for a divinity, and doubtless some never saw the light of day because the means were lacking.

At the same time, the Khmers did not abandon their indigenous deities, the masters of the land and its abundance, human heroes who became guardian spirits, and, of course, the protecting ancestors of each lineage. Evil spirits also roamed the land, bringing sickness or death. All these numerous and diverse divinities were worshipped, although doubtless with less complex rituals than those of the Indian gods, and similarly their shrines would generally have been simpler and mainly built of perishable materials, as are those which house them nowadays (see page 14). They were nevertheless of considerable importance in Khmer eyes and probably evoked much more dread than the Indian gods who were naturally more remote, if only because of their ability to inflict immediate retribution when they were annoyed. These divinities were thus probably the subject of more regular attention, but not a single shrine survives, nor even a description of their rituals – unless, of course, it has gone unrecognised. While there are occasional allusions to some of these divinities in the inscriptions they are, as it were, accidental, since none of the texts is specifically intended for them. This is why so little is known of the foremost local deity, the renowned *Devaraja*, or 'the god who is king', who was the counterpart of the Khmer 'king of kings'. Much ink has flowed on the subject of this divinity, in inverse proportion to the scanty and succinct references which exist in the actual documents. The next chapter will revert to the matter when the reign of Jayavarman II is described.

At the end of the twelfth century some short inscriptions occur which give the names of certain personages on the reliefs of Angkor Wat and those of the gods who inhabited the cellae of the temple complexes at the time. Sometimes, these inscriptions have been erased and replaced with others, which shows the mobility of the images. Occasionally they give the name of the donor of the statue, or that of the person on whom it was modelled. This type of information can also be found on the base of some of the bronze statues, and in rare cases the date of a statue's enshrinement in a temple is also given.

Stone Buddha under naga, *Angkor Wat style.*
(Sawanvaranayok museum, Thailand)

Right: The Hell of Maharaurava, southern gallery of bas-reliefs, Angkor Wat.

Far right: Shiva dancing from the pediment above the east entrance to the central sanctuary, Phnom Rung, north-east Thailand.

Opposite: A king prostrates himself in front of the statue of Vishnu, southern inner gallery, Bayon.

32-armed Lokeshvara, from the west side of the outer gallery, Banteay Chhmar.

Above: Meditating Shiva from the pediment above the east entrance pavilion, Phnom Rung, north-east Thailand.

Above left: Wild buffalo tethered for sacrifice, eastern outer gallery, Bayon.

Left: Unfinished bas-relief, showing a temple with three towers and linga, *south-east corner pavilion, Bayon.*

Opposite: Yama, the God of Death and Judgement, seated on a buffalo, southern gallery of bas-reliefs, Angkor Wat.

Rice-fields south-west of Phnom Bakheng.

Opposite: A princess being borne in a palanquin, southern gallery of bas-reliefs, Angkor Wat.

LIFE IN THE TEMPLES AND VILLAGES

What was life like in the temples? There are some inscriptions to which we have referred which suggest that life in the village in ancient days was not radically different from what it was in Cambodia as described in the late nineteenth century. Long lists of 'slaves' with their temple duties are engraved on the steles of some sanctuaries, for example at Preah Ko or Lolei. The existence of these 'slaves (of the god)' recorded as such on a sort of roll of honour is proof enough that a large proportion of villagers played an active role in the life of the temples, as they do today.

It should also be remembered that Hindu temples are not meeting-places in the same way as Christian churches, but residences of a god worshipped under a specific name, whose special mission is to safeguard the prosperity of the region entrusted to him, and whom priests have a duty to serve as they would serve a great nobleman.

Each morning, therefore, the god would be awoken, bathed, dressed and offered a meal. At midday they would return to feed him, and again in the evening, when additionally he would be prepared for his nightly repose. This was the duty of the temple priests. But at the same time musicians would come to charm him, cooks would be preparing the food, other servants would have the duty of making ready the leaves on which the dishes would be served, or would be husking the rice or weaving his flowers into garlands. Night guards were needed for the temple, guards for the treasury and guards for the various chambers, and farmers for the paddy fields which he owned and which provided the rice which was offered to him daily all year round. Of course, on festival days, the whole population gathered around the temple, necessitating even more ministers. All this for just one god, but in each great temple there were many more. At Preah Ko there were six principal deities, four at Lolei and 109 on the pyramid of Phnom Bakheng. In addition there were various numbers of all the minor divinities in these temples, who also needed to be attended to.

These were not full-time temple servants, as shown by their great numbers. For example, the north shrine of Lolei records a list of 182 people per fortnight as temple staff, and these are over and above the resident priests! It is thus an established fact that the local people used to take turns to serve the gods who governed the world order in general, and their own personal fate, in a rota system, to bear witness to their own faith. Beyond the temple, they attended to their daily needs. Festivals were quite often held throughout the year, but one was more important than the others. Each temple had its annual festival which was more or less sumptuous according to the means of the faithful. It was then that the god was taken from his cella on a procession around the temple, and of course everyone came to accompany and worship him and probably to solicit some personal favour.

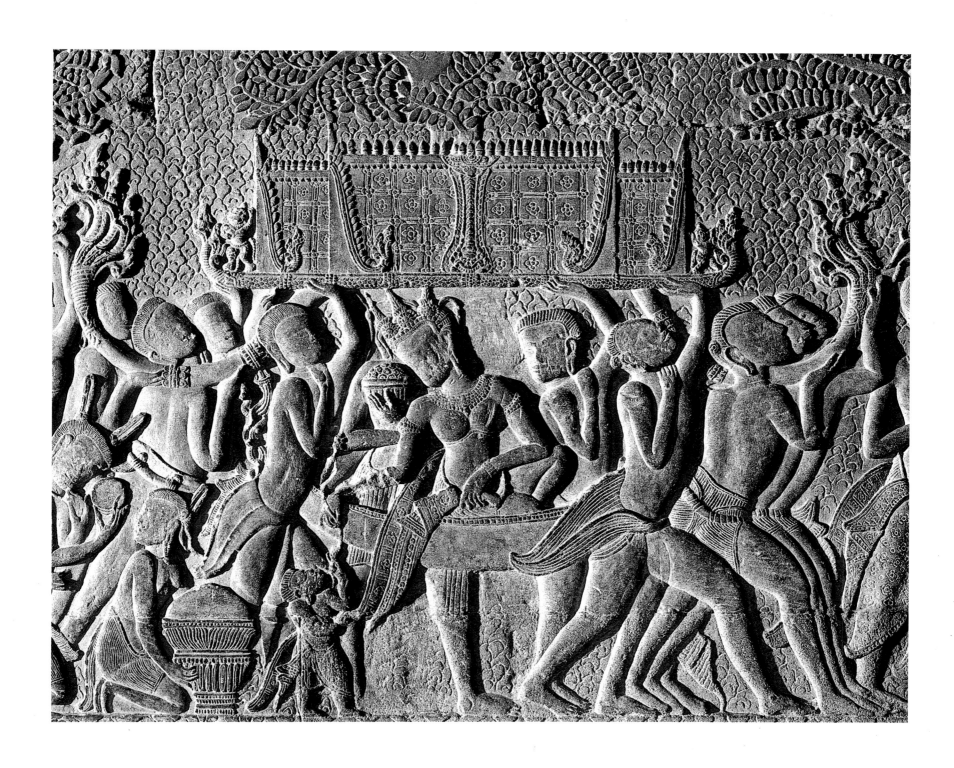

A corner of the moat, Angkor Wat.

Below: Spean Praptos, a bridge about 60 kms south-east of Angkor. (Photo: Guy Nafilyan)

Opposite: The main western entrance to Angkor Wat.

THE ARCHITECTURE

Right up to the present day, domestic dwellings have been built in traditional ways and predominantly of perishable materials. Naturally, nothing survives of the ancient houses except occasional finds of tiles, but recent excavations inside the royal palace of Angkor Thom have uncovered the base of massive wooden stakes which probably date from the beginning of the tenth century. However the reliefs indicate that the houses were not radically different from those we see today in the Khmer countryside, built on piles, or more precisely made of a structure of posts and beams to which a floor and walls were attached, and which supported the roof. The posts were chosen as far as possible from hard, rot-resistant woods. The floor and walls were made of various materials according to the owner's wealth; split or woven bamboo for the poorest, up to fine teak planks for the rich.

Similarly the roofs were made from 'straw hut grass' (*Imperata cylindrica* P. Beauv.), or from certain types of leaf, of woven coconut palm fronds, or of tiles. As Zhou Daguan writes at the end of the thirteenth century: "The dwellings of princes and high dignitaries have a quite different layout (from those of the royal palace) and different dimensions from the houses of the people. All the outer buildings have thatched roofs; only the family shrine and the main living quarters may have tiled roofs. The individual's official rank determines the dimensions of his dwelling. The common people use only thatch, and would not dare to have the smallest tile in their roof. The dimensions depend on a person's wealth but the people would never dare imitate the layout of the houses of the nobility".

There was also a splendid civil, military and religious infrastructure, with embanked roadways and bridges grouped with the ponds and temples around which the population lived. The urban planning was closely linked with admirable feats of civil engineering, focused especially on control of the water supply which was essential for survival.

This was what led the Khmers to create and exploit the *baray*, the sometimes huge reservoirs where water was stored within dikes and apportioned through a network of canals. The largest was the West Baray which covered an area of 1,760 hectares, and with a typical depth of 7 metres had a capacity of over 123 million cubic

Opposite: Satellite picture showing the layout of the main Angkor area with the West Baray, Angkor Thom and Angkor Wat clearly visible. (Photo: © CNES 1989, distribution SPOT image)

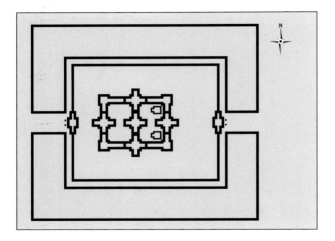

The plan of Ta Som temple showing the characteristic arrangement of the concentric moat, wall, gallery and central sanctuary.

Above: Aerial view of Angkor Wat looking towards the west.

Opposite: North-west corner of the central sanctuary of, Angkor Wat.

metres. Mention must also be made of the moats which surrounded temples and towns. The moats of Angkor Wat were 200 metres wide and around six kilometres in length and easily stored a great volume of water. With a typical depth of five metres they could store six million cubic metres. Those around Angkor Thom were longer and narrower, and had approximately the same capacity.

The main evidence for Khmer architecture, and ultimately for Khmer civilisation, however, remains the religious buildings, considerable in number and extremely varied in size. They were destined for the immortal gods, and as they were built of the durable materials of brick, laterite and sandstone, many have survived to the present day. They were usually surrounded by enclosures to protect them from evil powers, but confusion has often arisen as to which is a temple enclosure and which is that of the town of which the temple was a part.

To gain a proper understanding of what a Khmer temple was, it should first be recalled that it was not a meeting place for the faithful but the palace of a god, who was enshrined there to allow him to bestow his beneficence, in particular on the founder and his familiars. There was thus the need to build the finest possible residence for him, to be sure, although as he was there in the form of a statue there was little need for a large space. One of the largest is the central shrine of Angkor Wat and its cella has internal dimensions of 4.6 metres by 4.7; the pedestal of the statue being approximately the width of the door, would have been 1.6 metres square. So a great temple would not be a vast palace for a single god but a grouping of multiple shrines with a main divinity at the centre. Preah Khan temple, for example, was originally conceived to house more than 400 deities, and many others were to be added subsequently. The shrines could be linked or surrounded by galleries, which usually had doors and themselves housed certain divinities. In any case they were in no way intended to provide passage for great processions as has too often been asserted; such processions would have been greatly impeded, or rendered impossible by the doors and their disproportionately large thresholds. Some are not even accessible on foot, for example Ta Keo where it seems there was not even provision for doorways.

As the residence of a god, or gods, the sacred territory in which the temple is sited is a recreation of the universe inhabited by the gods with the centrally-placed Mount Meru their heavenly seat, surrounded by the primordial ocean. Thus the *prasat*, the sanctuary tower, usually represents Mount Meru and is often flanked by four subsidiary *prasats* arranged in a quincunx and echoing the five peaks of the sacred mountain. The various enclosures symbolize the mountains surrounding it, and the moat represents the ocean.

This world image, at least in the plan stage, was to impose a rigorous order of construction on Khmer architecture, from the simplest buildings to the most complex

Pilaster detail with kala *and* garuda, *Banteay Srei.*

Right page: In the foreground, a devata *on the east face of south tower; in the background, the south blind door of the central tower, Banteay Srei.*

monumental groups. In reality, as might be expected as long as a temple remained an active place of worship, the Khmers added smaller or greater numbers of extra shrines to the original coherent group – especially from the reign of Jayavarman VII onwards. This is particularly evident at Preah Khan, and the practice can result in an impression of chaos to the modern eye. It is not too difficult, however, to ascertain the original layout.

From Sambor Prei Kuk at the beginning of the seventh century to Angkor Wat in the twelfth century, the temples are designed in enclosures of quadrangular shape which centre on the main shrine, or on the central group of shrines, and are laid out according to a precise method. Geometrical rules, which probably varied according to the type of shrine, determine the siting and dimensions of each subsidiary group in relation to the centre of the temple and its sanctuary. But in the absence of written documents, there is no alternative but to retrace the original design a posteriori.

The order is marked too by the hierarchy of the elements of the overall plan. The central *prasat* is dominant, at least through its height, although not always its overall area, and the other elements are distributed around it according to their size and volume, so as to grant its full significance as the exact centre of the temple. The primacy of the central shrine is also emphasised by its elevation on a terrace of variable height, or in the case of the state temples, on a stepped pyramid. Hierarchical considerations also dictated the type and positioning of the decorative work. It is more profuse and richer on the central shrine which it sometimes covers entirely, and diminishes progressively in scope as it recedes from the centre. The most obvious example is Banteay Srei, where the three main shrines are richly decorated over their whole surface, with *dvarapala* carved on the central tower and *devata* on the north and south towers, whilst the preceding hall, linked by a screen or newel, is adorned with a patchwork of small squares in alternate patterns. The 'libraries' feature fine decoration on their main east and west faces, and have pediments which count among the most beautiful in Khmer art, but their sides are undecorated. The decoration becomes less profuse as it reaches the gate-lodges and ancillary buildings, up to the entry pavilion to the so-called fourth enclosure. An alternative explanation might be possible, namely that the original intention was to cover the whole temple with decorative carvings, beginning traditionally with the central shrine, and moving progressively outwards. Counter-examples would however be easy to adduce, and the reality is that, for one reason or another, not a single Khmer temple was actually 'completed'.

There are other conventions governing the design of Khmer monuments. In the case of the sanctuary towers, the superstructure features several storeys progressively reducing in height, superimposed on the central mass, and representing the successive concentric levels of Mount Meru. In the 'temple mountain' design such as at Pre Rup and Ta Keo, however, the pyramid is itself an image of Mount Meru, through the

ascending concentric universes of its superstructure, echoing those of the sanctuary towers. The elements which form the towers and the levels of the pyramid diminish progressively in size, producing the effect of "vertical soaring: a genuine optical illusion, a trick of perspective, which enhances the actual height".

These steadily diminishing proportions are also present in the miniature buildings nestling in the corners of each scaled-down level of the pyramid, like elements of an acroterium. An outstanding example, illustrating reduction in both scale and imagery can be seen in the northern group of monuments at Sambor Prei Kuk. On the east side of the central shrine's south face, there is a 'flying palace' – a kind of picture of a facade sculpted in brick. Every detail is present: the frame, the colonnettes, the lintel with its *makaras*, the pilasters and the pediment. The sculpted panel is about two metres high. At the top of this carved picture, in the tympanum of the pediment, is a miniature of the same 'flying palace', also sculpted in brick. The temple thus 'decorates itself' in its own likeness.

The inscriptions often mention the date, and sometimes the precise moment, at which a statue was 'brought to life' (the text speaks of "opening a statue's eyes"), which was the crucial instant in the life of the temple. There was no solemn ceremony for the inauguration of a temple on its completion (which would have been difficult to determine exactly), nor one for laying the first stone. We know, however, that the Indian *shastras* which laid down the rules of architecture, emphasised the extreme importance of the initial ceremonies for a building, and this is well attested by the presence of various 'foundation offerings' deposited beneath the actual foundations of the shrine, and also beneath the pedestals of the statues (which is why they have all been overturned by thieves), or even at the summit of the towers. The offerings were deposited in a square flagstone with various cavities, some of which were marked by letters and covered with a lid. In these cavities, precious stones, thin gold leaves, or even strands of hair or nail-clippings from the donor's body, were placed.

One final point is that the deity was not always a statue at the centre of the shrine, especially in the case of Shiva who, as supreme god, was most often represented by the *linga*, or phallus. Inserted in its pedestal, the *linga* in Khmer sculpture comprises three sections, and is a symbol of the Brahman trinity. Only the cylindrical top third was visible, sometimes ending in an ovoid shape, and representing Shiva. The middle section was octagonal and represented Vishnu, while the bottom third was square and symbolised Brahma. Both were hidden within the pedestal. As with the statues in the round, the pedestal was surmounted by a square stone slab with a central hole and a spout to allow the lustral water to run off and be collected by the faithful. When a *linga* is the central feature, this slab is called a *yoni*, a 'womb', which is a symbol of fertility and, by extension, prosperity.

Acroter in the form of a miniature temple, Banteay Srei style, 10th century. (Musée Guimet)

Left: The central sanctuary of Phimai in north-east Thailand. Its tower is the archetype of the Angkor Wat style.

Opposite above: A 'flying palace' from the pediment above the west door of the central sanctuary, Prasat Phnom Rung, north-east Thailand.

Opposite below: A 'flying palace' from Sambor Prei Kuk. (Photo: Guy Nafilyan)

SCULPTURE

Apart from the *linga*, there were numerous statues in the minor shrines, and occasionally in the principal one. They included Shiva, Vishnu, and occasionally Brahma. Ganesha occurs frequently, and there are statues of Skanda and many other deities, of which the female ones are not always easy to identify. In addition, there are sculptures of monsters: *kala*, *makara* and the omnipresent *naga*, often of monumental proportions. On a similar scale there are the guardians of the temple entrances: mainly *dvarapala* and mythical lions.

The bas-relief frieze carvings deserve special attention. The technique appears at an early period on the lintels and 'flying palaces' at Sambor Prei Kuk in the seventh century, and on the topmost level of the pyramid temple of Bakong in the ninth. The finest reliefs were to appear in the tenth century on the pediments of Banteay Srei temple and its 'libraries'. Less well-known are the relief-decorated panels on the walls of Bapuon (eleventh century), which have almost all tumbled down, or been taken down, and those of Prasat Khna Sen Kev, lost in a faraway forest. A century later there are further examples of relief-carved pediments at Angkor Wat, Banteay Samre and Beng Mealea. The great mural bas-relief friezes are at Angkor Wat, Bayon and Banteay Chhmar.

During the course of Khmer history, sculpture in the round appears to have begun with supple, naturalistic statues, and developed towards the stiff, conventional images of the late periods. The initial models seem to have been imported from India, perhaps as statuettes, but the sculptors, while following the Indian rules for portraying the suppleness of the body, also drew their inspiration from the real people around them and copied from nature. In the early period – the sixth and seventh centuries – they produced supple and lively statues, clad in naturalistic garments, such as the Phnom Da Vishnu, the Harihara from Prasat Andet and the 'lady' from Koh Krieng. It is possible to reproduce with today's Khmer garb – the *sampot* or the *krama* – the various folds portrayed on the statues of this ancient time.

Statues of a subsequent period become more and more rigid and conventionalised, as for example in the Koh Ker style of the first half of the tenth century. This was probably a result of formalism in the service of ritual significance, but there were variations along the way. While the general tendency was towards hardened, rigid icons, there were intervals of softer contours, doubtless due to the taste of individual artists, especially evident in the art of Banteay Srei and in a different guise, that of Bapuon.

This oscillation between the two tendencies is apparent in the style of Angkor Wat. The statues in the round are elegant and admirably proportioned, but tend towards rigidity, while one only needs to wander around the walls of the entrance

Stone linga *representing the essence of Shiva. Originally only the top third would be visible. Soong Noen, northeast Thailand.*

Opposite: The Khmer army in battle, eastern outer gallery, Bayon.

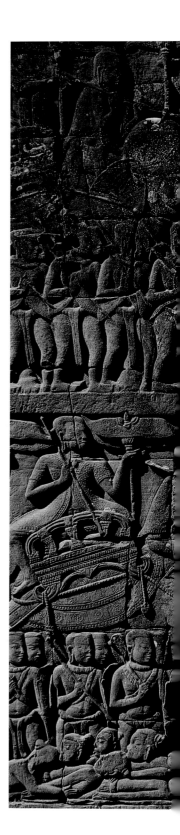

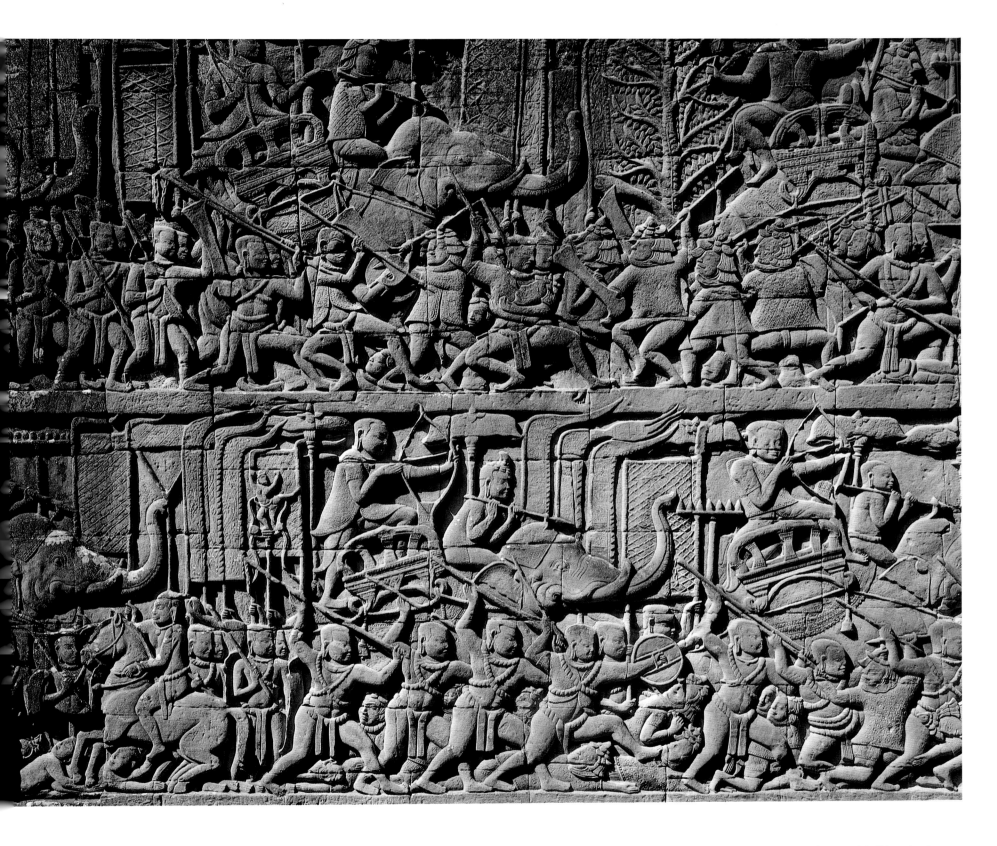

pavilions, or the 'libraries' and the galleries, to find the most charming *apsaras*, with their superb jewellery and coiffure, in a wide variety of supple attitudes. It is as though the sculptors, while bound by the sacred rules for carving the statues of divinities, gave free rein to their imagination when they embellished the temple walls with images of the royal ballerinas of the time.

The Bayon style was to bring new trends into play, at the turn of the thirteenth century. First of all there was a great increase in the number and extent of the religious building projects. The proliferation of sculptures resulted in a drop in their quality, as there was no corresponding increase in the numbers of good sculptors. But at the same time a new type of commission appeared: the portrait. Sculpture of the highest quality makes its reappearance in these portrait statues, as it does in that invention of genius, the 'towers carved with faces'. It is fortunate that seemingly the best sculptors were assigned to this supremely challenging task. A final innovation of the Bayon style is the depiction of everyday life on the relief friezes, side by side with the turmoil of the battles, and the scenes from the stories of the gods. Perhaps someone, someday, will make a special study of this 'cinema in stone' which unfolds along the walls of Bayon.

Bronze Prajñaparamita. (National Museum, Bangkok)

Right: Reclining Vishnu, Preah Khan. The god is here lying on a long-bodied dragon rather than the customary naga.

Above: The naga is one of the most ubiquitous features in Khmer architecture, appearing on pediments and balustrades throughout the kingdom over many centuries. This example comes from Banteay Srei.

Above left: A garuda corner antefix on an interior cornice of the 13th century Preah Khan. In Hindu mythology the garuda is the mortal enemy of the naga.

Left: A frieze showing a kala grasping a garland from Banteay Kdei. The kala, like the naga, is an iconographic element which continues from the early Khmer period onwards.

More than 2,000 apsaras *or* devatas *decorate the temple of Angkor Wat. Careful study reveals many differences in their dress, head-dresses and physiognomy.*

Chapter two
THE PRE-ANGKOR PERIOD

Khmer history is conventionally subdivided into three major phases. All three relate to Angkor and to the history of its kings during the middle period which, perhaps a little too precisely, is assigned the dates of 802-1431 AD. Thus we have the pre-Angkor period, characterised by considerable fragmentation with sporadic attempts at unification; the Angkor period – continuous exercise of power in Angkor – and the post-Angkor phase when the seat of power shifted to the region of Phnom Penh.

There is evidence however that settlements existed at Angkor from the very earliest times. There are few traces of neolithic sites, but an area so continuously settled and profoundly transformed by man could scarcely have retained them. Aerial photography of the zone around Angkor does reveal a considerable number of circular sites like the one identified long ago in Lovea village, which may well indicate very ancient habitation by peoples whose race and language remain unknown but whose neolithic origin is confirmed by finds of stone tools and ceramics.

There is rather more evidence from the seventh and eighth centuries of settlements which from then onwards are definitely Khmer. At that time the Angkor region was apparently the kingdom of Aninditapura, one of the many kingdoms and principalities which made up the land of the Khmers before the ninth century. History does not relate how many of these there were, and probably the number varied. We know some of their names from inscriptions but cannot guess their real importance.

Chinese chroniclers did however describe states in South-East Asia, and among these we have identified and approximately located two in the territory now known as Cambodia: Funan and Chenla. These names are presumably Chinese transliterations of local toponyms which are now hard to identify in ways which might establish a firm link between Chinese and indigenous sources.

Statue of Vajimukha, Pre Rup style 947-c.965, from Sambor Prei Kuk. (Musée Guimet)

Opposite: The doorway is all that remains of the north-east brick tower; behind, the central tower of Bakong.

Aerial view of Lovea village, an early circular site on the Angkor plain. (Photo: Guy Nafilyan)

Opposite: Three Sambor Prei Kuk-style lintels. Typical features are the large main garland with medallions disgorged by makaras, with smaller hanging pendants.

Above: Head of a 7th century Harihara statue in Phnom Da style, found at Ashram Maha Rosei, Phnom Da. (National Museum, Phnom Penh)

FUNAN

"The people of Funan are cunning and clever. They kidnap the citizens of nearby towns who do not pay them homage, and make them their slaves. Their merchandise is gold, silver and silk. The sons of prosperous families tailor brocade to make sarongs for themselves, and the women dress by pulling down a garment over their heads. The poor wrap themselves in a piece of cloth. The Funanese make cast gold rings and bracelets and silver dishes. They cut down trees to make their dwellings. The king lives in a storeyed pavilion. They surround their properties with wooden palisades. By the sea a tall bamboo grows, with leaves eight or nine feet long. These leaves are woven into roofs for the dwellings. The people also live in houses built on piles. They build boats which have a draught of eight or nine chang (ten Chinese feet). Their breadth is six or seven feet. The prow and the poop are like the head and tail of a fish. When the king travels, he does so on elephant back. For recreation, the people indulge in cockfights and pig fights." (*Nan Xichou*, trans. into French by Paul Pelliot).

These observations on Funan in the Chinese history entitled *Nan Xichou*, are believed to be the oldest in existence. It was located in the southern part of today's Vietnam and Cambodia, and seems to have been both a major South-East Asian state and one which was to become a constituent of the future Khmer empire. Apart from the remarks on the inhabitants' clothing and craft occupations, observed from lifestyles which were to characterise subsequent Khmer civilisation for a long period, the striking aspect of these Chinese records is their perception of the politics of the towns in the state of Funan. Their observation of continual struggles between kings, with the prospect of slavery for the losers, certainly creates a lasting impression. At the dawn of Khmer civilisation 'towns' were surrounded not by walls but by earth-banks combined with moats and probably surmounted by wooden palisades which were no doubt spiky. It is not unusual to find traces of these town moats in Cambodia or in north-east Thailand where a detailed study of them has been made. They are circular or quadrangular and enclose quite extensive areas. The village houses are all of wood and built on piles. Right until recent times the roofs have been thatched with woven coconut palm leaves. The boats were an essential feature of the Khmer landscape and have never been shaped like fish but like the mythical serpent, the *naga*.

As far as can be determined, the kingdom called Funan by the Chinese was a maritime state which at its zenith controlled the coast of the Gulf of Thailand from around the Mekong delta to the Isthmus of Kra. This made it highly attractive to both the Chinese and the Indians since the Kra region, on the Malay peninsula, was the zone of trans-shipment for both sides of the isthmus and thus a compulsory transit point for goods traded between India and the Far East. For this reason it was one of the first recipients of Indian civilisation probably towards the beginning of the

The base of the temple built by Mahendravarman at Wat Phu at the end of the 6th century – the oldest Khmer temple discovered to date. (Photo: Marielle Santoni)

Above: The mountain known as Lingaparvata on the west bank of the Mekong was chosen as the site of Wat Phu because of the natural linga *(just visible) on its summit. (Photo: Viengkéo Sanksavatdy)*

Christian era. Indian merchants would procure the goods they needed to trade with the Romans or their intermediaries in their own ports; particularly spices and other 'luxury goods' such as scented woods and aromatic resins. This Indo-Roman trade lasted until the weakening of the Roman Empire in the fifth century. As demand increased the Indians set up trading posts in South-East Asia, analogous to those established by the Europeans in India in the eighteenth century, with 'colonies' whose task was to gather the merchandise between monsoons. These expatriate merchants naturally brought with them their civilisation, their religion and their gods, which the natives gradually adopted. This was not at all a 'colonisation' as is understood today; the Khmers were never 'Indianised' in the full sense, as has been claimed, since they never abandoned their own civilisation.

Towards the 6th century, when the first inscriptions are attested, a legend was in circulation, recorded in almost the same form by the Chinese and a little later by the Chams. An Indian Brahmin named Kaundinya had a dream and made the voyage to Funan where he met and married Soma, the daughter of the serpent-king of the country, and brought Funan 'civilisation'. While it is a fact that all known kings before the ninth century claimed to be descendants of this primordial couple it would be quite illusory to seek historical truth in this legend. It is also invoked both in India and (according to Herodotus) as far away as Scythia, to explain the origin of a dynasty.

Towards the end of the sixth century, the Chinese annals write of a kingdom they call 'Chenla' which seems to correspond to one of the kingdoms in the interior of the Khmer country. Local inscriptions yield further and more precise information and although the Chinese used 'Chenla' until recent times as their name for Cambodia, we propose to drop it in favour of the epithets in the local texts.

BHAVAPURA: A POWERFUL KINGDOM APPEARS

The second half of the sixth century witnessed the founding of a city, Bhavapura, named as custom dictated after its founder, King Bhavavarman I. He was a prince from the region of Wat Phu in southern Laos. He had not been chosen as successor to the throne of his father's small state and decided, nevertheless, to carve out a kingdom of his own. Having conquered part of the centre of what is now Cambodia, he had established his capital some 30 kilometres from the town now called Kompong Thom. The precise location of his city, near or on the site of Sambor Prei Kuk, has not yet been identified.

Bhavavarman's conquests extended his kingdom for a considerable distance; he left an inscription north of the town of Battambang. Meanwhile his younger brother Citrasena who had been chosen as his father's successor was crowned king under the name of Mahendravarman and led expeditions to what is now north-east Thailand, making conquests as far as a point beyond the town of Khon Kaen. On his way he left triumphal inscriptions, but for unknown reasons he completely abandoned the land he had conquered and returned to take up residence at Bhavapura some years after 598 AD, following the death of his brother which he may have instigated.

Mahendravarman died around 610 AD leaving the throne to his son Isanavarman I who, in common with all Khmer kings and as a self-imposed duty, attempted to enlarge his kingdom by new conquests. It is thought that he became dominant over almost the whole of what is now Cambodia and that he pushed on through the pass north of Battambang to the sea, in the region of Chanthaburi in Thailand.

He was a great king, and the memory of him lived on down the ages; he is mentioned in a Bayon inscription of the 12th century. He was probably not very young when he assumed power. Posterity records his reputation for great wisdom. He will be remembered above all as the builder of his state temple: the 'southern group' of Sambor Prei Kuk which is one of the most ancient surviving examples of Khmer architecture. It is an extensive site of brick towers, in a double enclosure with exterior dimensions of 260 x 236 metres. Today there only remain seven sanctuary towers and part of the inner wall. The location of some of the other towers and gate-lodges can be traced, especially the east gate which has jambs inscribed with a text celebrating the glory of the King-builder. The central sanctuary is a magnificent, massive rectangular tower, its outer walls decorated with relief carving. To the east is a tower containing a striking sandstone pedestal intended for the bull Nandi, Shiva's inseparable companion, which is now missing but may have been cast in bronze. The renowned octagonal towers once soared in a quincunx but are now in ruins. The inner boundary wall was decorated with numerous relief medallions of which little remains. The scenes are merely sketched in broad outline as the brick would have had an outer coating, but from what remains one can imagine the splendour of the original group.

On the death of King Isanavarman I in 628 AD one of his younger sons succeeded under the name of Bhavavarman II. He was far from having the prestige of his father, and failed to maintain the unity of his empire. The princedoms regained their independence. One of these was situated in the north of the province now known as Kompong Thom. It was apparently of little importance and its name remains unknown but it was here that a prince was born who would rebuild the empire of Isanavarman I, whose grandson he was, under the name of Jayavarman I.

The 7th century Phum Phon, in Prei Kmeng style, is one of the earliest surviving Khmer temples, north-east Thailand.

The central tower in the southern group of sanctuaries at Sambor Prei Kuk. (Photo: Guy Nafilyan)

JAYAVARMAN I AND THE KINGDOM OF ANINDITAPURA

The earliest recorded date in the reign of Jayavarman I was Wednesday 14 June 657 AD. On that day two shrines were consecrated in places a considerable distance away from each other; one in the north of present-day Battambang province and the other in Prei Veng province in south-east Cambodia. According to the inscriptions both their founders acknowledged the supremacy of King Jayavarman I, so by that date the king must have almost completed his reconquest.

Jayavarman's capital, like that of the god Indra, was named Purandarapura. For a long time it was thought to have been in the south of today's Cambodia since it is there that most of the inscriptions mentioning the king have come to light. It is significant nevertheless that he did not directly commission the engraving of any of the texts discovered so far, even when they reproduce various edicts of his. At a time when there was quite considerable activity in the building of shrines, not one can be definitely attributed to him. Such uncertainty about the monuments of someone who remained in the memory of the Khmers as a very great king, gives rise to speculation, and there are good arguments indeed to sustain a different hypothesis.

Jayavarman I could scarcely have wanted to the rule the empire from the seat of his father in the north of Cambodia, well away from the centre, but the south too was just as remote. Not far from Angkor, however, there are distinct vestiges of the king and this prompts the speculation that he might have chosen that region, which was then the kingdom of Aninditapura, to establish his capital.

The kingdom was probably by then quite sizeable although the name of Aninditapura itself only appears later in the inscriptions of the Angkor period. It seems however that as well as the Angkor region it included that of Roluos to the west, and extended as far as the north and north-western parts of present-day Battambang province. The capital city which would probably have given its name to the kingdom has never been found nor located in maps but it is attested in the inscriptions. If our hypothesis holds good, it was replaced by Jayavarman I's Purandarapura and then presumably by the capitals which we describe below: Hariharalaya founded in the course of the 8th century, and Yashodharapura at its end.

Above: This lintel from Bakong has many interesting iconographic details. Makaras *with riders disgorge* simhas *which support the central garland.*

Left: Fragment of a bas-relief from Bakong showing a battle between the gods and asuras. *That the* asuras *were beaten can be seen from the broken standard.*

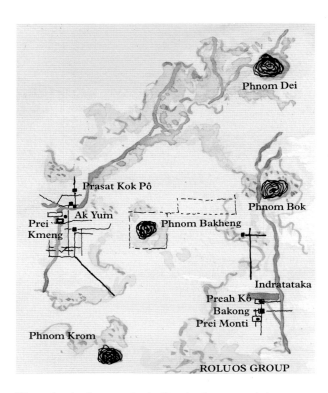

The entire Angkor area in the Pre-Angkorean period.

THE FIRST TEMPLE MOUNTAIN: AK YUM

One of the most impressive pre-Angkor vestiges in the Angkor region is the temple of Ak Yum. It was rediscovered only in 1932 as it had been partially buried under the south embankment of the West Baray while the latter was under construction. In its restored state it is the first real temple mountain known. It consists of a three-storey brick pyramid with five towers in quincunx on the upper terrace. It is assigned to the second half of the 8th century but the names both of the king who first built it and the one who modified it are unknown. The problem is a source of some frustration as the latter in particular must surely have been a powerful and ambitious ruler to carry out this considerable project, but the historical data of the period do not allow us to guess who he might have been. We do not know precisely how the former temple might have looked but an inscribed door-jamb was re-used in the main sanctuary door, which shows how important it was to the builder; it carries a date corresponding to Saturday 10 June 674 AD. Around Prasat Ak Yum a number of other sites of some size have been identified and seem to be of the same period.

The temple was built in the centre of a square enclosure, parts of which are still visible, and which may have been two kilometres square. It is possible too that the open right-angled dike clearly visible to the west of the West Baray, with branches which to this day are over a kilometre long, was one of the mysterious king's achievements. Such a system collects rainwater or water from streams flowing between its branches and was possibly already in use at Sambor Prei Kuk. It probably predates the building of the *baray*.

Jayavarman I certainly takes his place alongside Isanavarman I as one of the dominant personalities of the pre-Angkor period. His death probably occurred shortly before 700 AD. His immediate successor may have been his son-in-law Nripaditya whose short reign brought his spouse Jayadevi to the throne on his demise. She was a daughter of Jayavarman, and there is a definite reference to her in the region in 713 AD. She is the only known female sovereign in ancient Khmer history. It seems however that Nripaditya and Jayadevi did not extend their rule beyond the kingdom of Aninditapura itself, though there may have been a small enclave in the south of Cambodia. The rest of the country reverted to small fragmented kingdoms with only the larger ones being known by name.

This state of affairs was to last for the whole of the 8th century, but despite the political fragmentation and our ignorance of even the major events of the period, we should not conclude that a state of anarchy or cultural impoverishment prevailed. On the contrary, the 8th century is credited with fine examples of Khmer sculpture, notably the Harihara statue of Prasat Andet, and with monuments of high quality albeit on a small scale.

Jayavarman II: 'World Emperor'

In 790 AD a young prince became king, taking the name of Jayavarman II. He was a descendant of the great family of Khmer kings whose lineage went back to the princes of Aninditapura. He had come from 'Java' where he is assumed to have been 'held prisoner' with his family. In fact the name Java denotes a country whose identity is disputed. It may have lain in the region of present-day Malaysia but it was probably not the island of Java itself. Jayavarman II assumed power in the kingdom of Vyadhapura in the general area of the town now called Prei Veng in south-east Cambodia. One of his first tasks was to have a religious ceremony performed to free him from the tutelage of the 'King of Java'. From this it has been deduced that the latter was the 'suzerain' of the Khmer country, or at least of a considerable part of its territory. At the same time or soon afterwards Jayavarman seized the kingdom of Shambupura, today's Sambor, south of Kratie. As his capital he chose Indrapura, a site quite plausibly identified with present-day Banteay Prei Nokor. Although not rich in monuments it is marked out by a two and half kilometre-square earth-bank, which in fact lies at the presumed frontier between the two kingdoms about 40 kms south-east of Kompong Cham town.

Pursuing his conquests northwards he reached Wat Phu in southern Laos, where there was a shrine which had long been worshipped by the Khmer kings. He then made his way along the southern range of the Dangrek mountains and finally took the kingdom of Aninditapura, settling in its capital Hariharalaya somewhere in the region of Roluos. He probably intended to extend his rule even further westwards and to this end he attempted to found a new capital, Amarendrapura, on a site which remains unknown. But he must have experienced a setback from the kings he had dispossessed or reduced to vassal status. We know that, for whatever reason, he abandoned the capital, fled and took refuge in a town east of Angkor on the summit of Mahendraparvata, the 'mountain of the great Indra', which is today called Phnom Kulen. It overlooks the region of Angkor for which it serves as a watershed. It was here that in 802 AD, probably to assert his power in the face of his adversaries despite the odds, he had himself crowned as *chakravartin* – 'world emperor'. This date is imprinted in the memory of the Khmers as marking the foundation of their empire.

The stele of Queen Jayadevi (K904) dated 713 AD.

THE DEVARAJA CULT

At the same time Jayavarman II caused a wise Brahmin to evoke a Khmer god whose status could correspond to that which he had newly attributed to himself. In every Khmer kingdom there was a parallel king of the tutelary spirits of the land, co-ruling with the earthly monarch. As Jayavarman had established himself as 'supreme king of kings', he naturally had to raise a divine counterpart from the empire's guardian spirits. This is what he did, using the title *Kamrateng Jagat ta Raja:* the 'god who is king' (translated in Sanskrit by *devaraja*). This *devaraja* title has been misunderstood and has given rise to much speculation, for example that it denotes Shiva, or another god deemed to be the essence of the supreme Khmer king, who then was mistakenly considered to be a 'god-king'.

To this divinity Jayavarman attached a priest, decreeing that the latter's descendants would thenceforth be exclusively empowered to conduct the rituals of worship. In fact the existence of the *devaraja,* like that of so many other local guardian spirits, would never have been known had it not been for one of the priest's descendants who was still fulfilling the ritual functions two and a half centuries later, combining them with his duties as tutor to king Udayadityavarman II. The position enabled him to provide handsomely for the temple of his priestly line, which until then had been of modest proportions, in Sdok Kok Thom near Aranyaprathet in Thailand. Its designation and history are revealed on the engraved stele from the site (see page 64).

The unanswered question is: when did Jayavarman decide he was strong enough to descend from the mountain and return to take up his seat in Hariharalaya, where he would die in about 835 AD? The closing years of his reign were apparently very peaceful. Having proclaimed himself king of the Khmer kings, it seems curious that he did not seek to extend his sway over the kingdoms he had not conquered, for example those in the south-west of today's Cambodia.

Although for the Khmers he had been the prestigious founder of the empire it has long been problematic to attribute to him the building of even a single temple. However Rong Chen, a three-tiered four-sided pyramid about 100 metres square at its base seems to have been his work. In its present state it is anything but spectacular. It is perched on one of the highest points of Phnom Kulen and could have been the scene of Jayavarman's consecration as king. The rather inelegant shape of the monument could be due to the haste with which it was built. Apart from Rong Chen, a number of other shrines are attributed to his reign but it is also possible that they were built by prominent dignitaries. They include most of the temples on Phnom Kulen and conceivably Preah Theat Thom and Preah Theat Toch within the enclosure of Jayavarman's first capital Banteay Prei Nokor, though not at its centre. In

the Roluos group it is more difficult to determine whether some temples belong to his reign or that of his son. Lastly, the shrine at Sambor Prei Kuk known as 'group C' in the centre has been attributed to the period. It is nevertheless probable that at that time the kingdom of Bhavapura was independent and that Jayavarman II was therefore unconnected with this edifice.

Everything we know of this king is gleaned from the epigraphy of succeeding ages; so much so that some historians think he became a legend soon after his death and thus was awarded highly exaggerated significance. The evidence, however, is that by the end of the 9th century he was already greatly venerated.

His son succeeded him under the name of Jayavarman III. From his reign only two accounts survive: both concern a white elephant hunt and one of them recounts a miraculous event. Should it be concluded from the lack of historical evidence that his reign was uneventful? Such concerns apart, he is credited with Prei Monti temple, which although of modest proportions stands in a large enclosure which could also have accommodated a palace. The fine tower of Trapeang Phong, also in the Roluos group, was probably built during this period. The latest discoveries could well cause us to revise our opinion of Jayavarman III. It is now known that the temples of Bakong and Preah Ko, which were assumed to be foundations commissioned by Indravarman I, Jayavarman's successor, were built on the precise site of earlier shrines.

Jayavarman III's successor acceded as late as 877 AD and as we do not know the date of the king's demise it is tempting to suppose that by then he had already been dead for some time, since it is hard to believe that such a seemingly insignificant prince could have reigned for more than 40 years while leaving so few traces to posterity. There were however to be similar instances in subsequent Khmer history and the new discoveries being made could well lead to a revised view of Jayavarman III and his achievements.

The Sdok Kok Thom stele (K235) is interesting for the information its give us about the devaraja *cult and its priests. (National Museum, Bangkok)*

The three eastern towers of Preah Ko. Their entrances are guarded by lion statues.

INDRAVARMAN I: THE FIRST MAJOR WORKS AT ANGKOR

Thus in 877 the supreme throne was assumed by King Indravarman I, a prince of somewhat obscure origin. The circumstances of his accession are shrouded in mystery, as he was unrelated to any previous king. He was probably no longer young on his accession and it is assumed he had gained most of his empire before receiving the title of 'supreme king' of the Khmer kings. In the year of his accession he commissioned inscriptions asserting his authority from the south of Cambodia, on Phnom Bayang temple, to the far north-east of present-day Thailand.

In a reign of some ten years he was to carry out major works, often of a pioneering nature. He does not seem to have felt the need for a physical enclosure of

Dvarapala in niche, Preah Ko.

the capital unless there was one which has since disappeared completely. His hydraulic engineering began with the first version of the Indratataka reservoir which is a sort of precursor of the great *baray* which were to enhance the wealth of Angkor and the major towns of the Khmer empire. Instead of closing off a valley by means of a large, right-angled open dike as for example Jayavarman I had done, he created a U-shaped dike 3,800 metres long from east to west, and 750 metres on the two shorter north-south sides. This 'tank', which remained open to the north, could collect the waters of several streams flowing more or less year-round from Phnom Kulen. As such, it was already the most ambitious hydraulic project ever to have been carried out in the country of the Khmers, but even at that time it was probably part of a grander plan, to judge from the 'island' which Indravarman had contrived at its centre. Indravarman, however, did not have time to close the dike off to the north, and we shall see that his son, Yashovarman I was to do so in some haste. Simultaneously Indravarman transformed at least one section of the Roluos river into a canal to facilitate the flow of water into the tank. These works also doubtless allowed for easier transit to his capital of the large quantities of sandstone which he was the first to use extensively in building his monuments.

On 25 January 880, Indravarman I held the rituals to dedicate the principal gods of Preah Ko temple, built to honour and propitiate the spirits of his kingly predecessors who were the natural guardians of the land over which they had held sway, and in particular the spirit of Jayavarman II. This small but quite outstanding temple stands in the eastern part of a large space enclosed by a rectangular moat measuring 500 metres in length by 400 metres in breadth. It bears no trace of other monuments and has not been excavated, but it could well have housed the palace of Indravarman I.

Preah Ko temple consists principally of a group of six tower-shrines in two rows of three, all built on a single sandstone base. The middle tower of the front row, slightly displaced towards the west in relation to the other two, was dedicated to Paramesvara 'the supreme lord', one of Shiva's names, and also in this case the posthumous title of Jayavarman II. He was flanked to the north by Rudresvara, the apotheosis of King Rudravarman, Indravarman's maternal grandfather, and to the south by Prithivindesvara fulfilling the same role for his father, King Prithivindavarman. The implication is that Indravarman I had brought under his rule the domains of these three kings at least. Another significant fact is that these three divinities, all with names which could be variants of that of the god Shiva, were symbolised not as might be expected by a *linga* but in the form of statues. The rear towers are smaller and apparently were dedicated to the chief queen of each monarch, worshipped under the names of goddesses.

Bakong: The State Temple

The final enterprise of Indravarman I was to build his state temple now known as Bakong. It was a sacred compound of considerably greater extent than what now remains. The pyramid we see today is actually at the centre of a square roughly 800 metres by 800. It would seem to be the largest sacred area ever delineated by the Khmers. Moreover the fact that it has two moats would suggest that they enlarged the area in a subsequent project, particularly in view of the unfinished state of the outer moat which lacks a gate-lodge, or at least one built of durable materials. The temple also features several innovations including the moats and the abundant use of sandstone.

It seems that during this reign that the innovation of surrounding temples with moats seems to have emerged. It was to become a regular practice and its symbolic significance has long been emphasised, but there was also an economic dimension. It should be noted that of the two concentric moats around Bakong, the outer one provided about fifteen hectares of water and the inner another twelve, amply justifying the epithet 'tank-moats' which is sometimes given them. With a mean depth of three metres they had a potential capacity of 810,000 cubic metres. Moreover the inner moat was faced throughout with stairways, obviously intended as ablution facilities for the faithful but where one can also imagine the local ladies drawing water for their domestic needs.

At least two broad avenues ran from the outer moat, one eastwards – it can still be followed for more than 500 metres – and one northwards ending at the Indratataka. The westward avenue was certainly shorter and it is uncertain whether there was ever one leading south as the moat does not seem to have a breach on that side. These avenues pre-date the construction of Preah Ko, leading us to believe that they were part of a sanctuary built prior to Bakong but probably on the same site.

Between the outer and inner moats there were 21 brick shrines of very similar design, and built at quite regular intervals. They were apparently the work of high officials, and not all of them were actually completed. In addition, in each angle there were two ponds 60 metres square which straddled a further tower, but only the north-eastern one was completed. The whole group is in an advanced state of dilapidation.

The inner 'tank-moat' was surrounded by a low wall punctuated by gate-lodges at each cardinal point. Only those to the east and west, which are incidentally the most elaborate, give access to the interior. They lead on to a causeway between massive stone *nagas* which are, unusually, at ground level. The inner enclosure wall is also low, and partially ruined. It encloses an area measuring 160 by 120 metres and between it and the tank-moat there is a 40-metre zone which could have accommodated living quarters, perhaps those of the temple ministers. Nowadays there is a pagoda which has probably long stood there.

Five-headed nagas *adorn the ends of one of the lintels from Preah Ko.*

In the middle of the inner enclosure which had four gate-lodges (all of which have since vanished) the central pyramid rises. It was surrounded by eight brick towers. Of the eastern pair little remains except their double sandstone base. The northern of the two seems to have housed a large statue of Vishnu and the southern, one of Shiva. Unusually each god was flanked by two of his wives. The towers to the north and south had substantial brick bases while the western ones were smaller than the others. At the four angles there are massive brick buildings conventionally termed 'libraries'. Those to the east are in pairs. Two north-south 'elongated galleries' in laterite along the east wall, and two others in sandstone were added in the twelfth (or as late as the 13th) century. The latter were westward extensions of small shrines, and the northern gallery housed a fine stele.

The central five-stepped pyramid is the major monument of this holy site. Faced entirely with sandstone, the imposing 'temple mountain', measures 65 metres by 67 at the base. The uppermost platform is 20 metres long by 18 wide and is 14 metres above ground level. It could well have been built around an earlier brick shrine.

Access to the summit is via four stairways, each step shallower than the one above to give the impression that the monument appears higher than it really is. This contrivance was to occur again in later buildings. At the base of each stairway there was a statue of Nandi, Shiva's 'vehicle', and an unusually shaped miniature sandstone temple decorated in low relief.

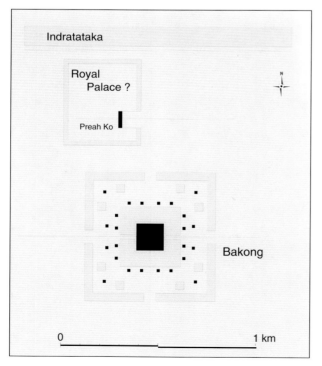

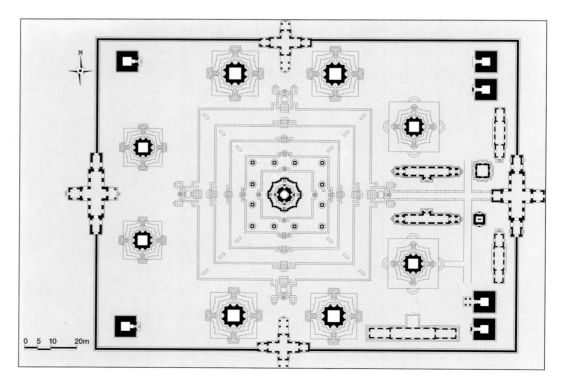

At the angles of the pyramid's first three terraces there were stone elephant-guardians of the 'intermediary points'. On the fourth terrace there are twelve small towers, one marking each angle and two others on each cardinal side. The latter may be the shrines dedicated to the eight 'forms' of Siva mentioned in the stele. The wall of the fifth terrace was covered with bas-relief carvings almost a metre high. What little remains attests to their great quality. A single south-facing stone showing the combat between the gods and the *asuras* has survived the ravages of erosion (see page 59).

Of the main sandstone shrine crowning the pyramid only the base remains. It is possible that the tower vanished or was badly damaged during the disturbances over Indravarman's succession. All that is known is that it was built of sandstone and that the god Indresvara enshrined there was consecrated in 881 AD.

Whatever the original construction might have been, there is nowadays a fine sandstone tower built two and a half centuries later in archaic style but with shapes and decoration closely akin to those at Angkor Wat. At some unknown date it collapsed but it was fully and admirably reconstructed in the late 1930s by Maurice Glaize, thanks to his great skill in matching the scattered stones, jigsaw-puzzle fashion.

The latest attested date for Indravarman I is 886 AD. It appears on an inscription discovered some 70 kilometres north-west of Ubon in Thailand, which also relates that the donor of a Buddhist statue in this far-away place formally recognised the authority of the king. Indravarman I died in 889 at the latest, perhaps a year or two earlier. It has hitherto been supposed that there was a smooth transition of power, since the throne was inherited by one of his sons. In fact this was not the case.

Two devatas *from the south-east corner of the central sanctuary, Bakong.*

Left: Inscription from Bakong, dated 881.

Opposite above: The southern brick tower of the western pair, Bakong.

Opposite far left: Plan showing the arrangement of moats and sanctuaries around Bakong and the relationship between it and Preah Ko. The small squares represent sanctuary towers, while the blue areas are moats and ponds.

Opposite left: Plan showing the central part of Bakong temple.

Overleaf
The eastern approach to the pyramid of Bakong passes between two distinctive, long stone halls. The central tower is in later Angkor Wat style.

Chapter three

THE FIRST ANGKOR

The end of the reign of Indravarman I (after 886 AD) was marked by a bitter power struggle, a circumstance which was to arise frequently in the following centuries. Apparently it was between brothers and it ended in victory for Yashovardhana. It featured a naval battle on the Great Lake, echoed in an inscription: "In his victorious march he destroyed myriads of ships which had appeared from all sides of the vast ocean …" While the combat was assuredly fierce it was apparently confined to the area of the capital and the royal palace of Hariharalaya. A significant outcome was the destruction of the palace, and it is likely too that the war resulted in the ruining of the main shrine of Bakong temple after it had been profaned by bloodshed.

The only recorded name is that of the victor, Yashovardhana, son of Indravarman I and Queen Indradevi. He had not been his father's designated crown prince: on the contrary it was through his mother that his main claim on the empire arose. He had himself crowned supreme king of the Khmer kings in 811 *saka* (between April 889 AD and April 890, most probably in 889) taking the name of Yashovarman – 'he who has Renown as his protector'.

At that time the king was doubtless in his prime. In all probability his father had been a king before he seized supreme power at Harihalaya and thus was quite advanced in age when he died. It is a plausible supposition that Yasovarman I was at least 30 at that time, that he had already been entrusted with a governorship – perhaps that of the land where his future capital would be established – and that he had had to curb his impatience while he endured his father's rule. Moreover he is praised in several inscriptions as an athlete of extraordinary strength. For example, it is recorded that "with a single stroke of his sword he cleft a large heavy copper bar into three pieces". Other verses convey the impression that he used to provoke his companions to fights from which he is glorified as always emerging the victor.

Statue of female divinity, Bakheng style c.907. (Musée Guimet)

Opposite: Relief carvings in brick of Vishnu's consort, Lakshmi, interior of the northern tower of Prasat Kravan.

Central detail of a simha *and* nagas *from a lintel at Lolei.*

Opposite above: Map of the Angkor area during the reign of Yashovarman I.

Opposite below: Stucco detail from the south-west tower, Lolei.

THE *ASHRAMAS*

In the same *saka* year 811 Yashovarman I also found time to have about 100 *ashramas* established throughout his empire, near the existing shrines. *Ashrama* is a Sanskrit word often translated as 'hermitage', and the contemporary word *'ashram'* which can often indicate something quite different, is derived from it. Yashovarman's *ashramas* housed probably quite small communities of holy people who wished to withdraw from the world.

Evidently for the new king the point in showing such an interest in the old shrines was to impress upon his vassals that he intended henceforth to be master of the whole of his father's empire. It is evident too that this was not the sole means he had of imposing his will, albeit the only one to have left a lasting record, thanks to the inscriptions.

Some twenty steles marking sites of these *ashramas* have been found. Apart from a genealogy and a panegyric for the king, they contain a set of rules of behaviour for prospective visitors and thus hint at whom the latter might have been, thereby giving a glimpse of Khmer society. For example entry to the ashrama was not allowed unless the visitor wore white garments and was otherwise unadorned – even sunshades were forbidden. The punishments for breaking the rules are listed according to rank. The 'king's sons' had to pay 20 *pala* (about 750 grams) of gold; ordinary people only three quarters of a *pala*, which was still a considerable sanction. If the latter could not pay they were given 100 strokes of the cane. Other fines were prescribed for priests who failed to observe the timetable and for temple servants who neglected their duties.

These steles are identical, so much so that they have been called 'posters in stone'. They are of considerable interest for the idea they give of the extent of Yashovarman's empire. They have been discovered in the extreme south of present-day Cambodia (but not in Vietnam), in the north near Wat Phu in Laos, in the region of Phnom Rung and in the province of Chanthaburi in Thailand. It is significant however that none have so far been discovered in central Cambodia near Sambor Prei Kuk which leads to the supposition that the kingdom of Bhavapura had remained independent.

The inscriptions are the only remaining traces of the *ashramas*, which were certainly of wood and so have perished. Their main characteristic is that they are digraphic, that is each of the two sides is engraved with the same Sanskrit text of 50 verses in two different scripts. The first is in traditional Khmer writing while the second, which did not survive beyond Yashovarman's reign, seems to have been specially made by royal command and based on a north Indian script with a considerable number of modifications, since an exact prototype in India itself has not been found.

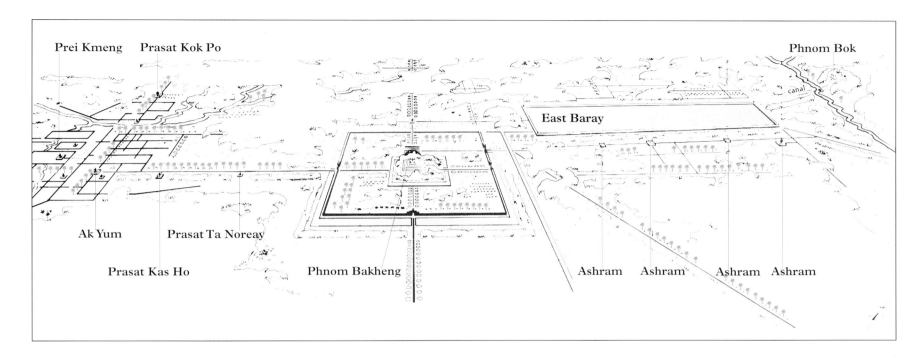

Apart from the script, surprising in itself, and which the king later tried in vain to enforce, it is notable that these inscriptions and others of the period show a quality of Sanskrit poetry which bears witness to a much higher level of culture than that which appears in similar texts of earlier periods. It would seem that these two characteristics could only have resulted from the influence of Indian scholars living in the Khmer court, but there is no other trace to indicate their arrival or presence there.

THE MOVING OF THE CAPITAL

The king had clearly marked out the extent of his empire and in their hyperbolic style the inscriptions describe him as "the supreme master of the Land whose borders stretch from the *Sukshmaka* and the *Amrataka* (probably tribes living in the Cardamom mountains of whom nothing else is known) to the ocean, China and Champa." Next he decreed a massive works project to found a new capital. In all likelihood the war of succession had destroyed his father's palace and even profaned the state temple so the way was clear for him to abandon the old capital Hariharalaya, which in any case may in his judgement have been incapable of the sort of development he had in mind. It can be surmised too that he was already well acquainted with the region which was to become Angkor and my suggestion is that he could well have had a degree of authority there before assuming the supreme throne

Devata in niche on the north-west tower of Lolei temple.

and have had long-standing plans to develop it. In any case his project was one of the most ambitious even undertaken there by the Khmer kings and he clearly wished to outdo the considerable achievements of his father in his own capital.

THE TEMPLE OF THE FAMILY ANCESTOR SPIRITS – LOLEI

Yashovarman I did not actually desert the Hariharalaya region for it was he who built the north dike of the Indratataka *baray* at the beginning of his reign. His father had created the other three sides and had provided for the positioning of the central 'island' which was to be a feature of all subsequent *baray*. Furthermore it can be seen that while the 'island' is in the exact centre of the pond in the east-west axis, it is clearly off-centre to the north along the north-south axis. It is obvious too that the proportions of the *baray* are unusual in being too narrow for its length. This leads to the conclusion that its builder originally intended it to be broader, as shown by the sitting of the island. If the distance between the latter and the south dike is doubled so as to find the breadth first sought, it comes to approximately 1,100 metres which give the *baray* similar proportions to others of its type. However the original plans were not taken up by Yashovarman, who wanted to use the 'island' to build a temple to the memory of his parents. To do this he needed to close off the north side of the *baray*, but he refused to widen it as intended, since he had already decided to move the capital.

The shrine on the 'island', known today as Lolei – a name which probably recalls the old Hariharalaya – consists in the main of four brick towers whose gods, dedicated to the spirits of his parents, were ritually consecrated on Sunday 8 July 893. Two and a half months beforehand he had made a major donation to two of the three gods of Preah Ko temple, who were also guardians of the land. Curiously enough Rudresvara (Rudravarman, the father of his paternal grandmother) was left out, leading to the conjecture that that particular king's domain had reverted to independence.

The 'island' is visible today as a large terrace 90 metres by 80 which accommodated an *ashrama* as well as the shrine surrounded by a brick wall with four gate lodges which have all disappeared. The arrangement of the four main towers which are square, six by six metre buildings is strangely asymmetrical. The north towers are precisely in the east-west axis of the terrace and there seems little doubt that this indicates that here, as at Preah Ko, the original intention was to have six towers in rows of three. As the stele which recounts this royal foundation mentions only four gods, the implication is that when it was carved the decision had already been taken not to build the two towers which would normally have been sited to the north to honour the guardians of a kingdom which Yashovarman coveted but which he had not succeeded in conquering. Entry to the island, according to the inscription, was through the north dike where there was a gate 'facing four ways', meaning it had four entrances. It was probably built of perishable materials since nothing remains. Apart from the fact that this was the shortest way to the island (entry was conventionally from the east), the reason for this anomaly could be that the king had created a dike-causeway from his new capital to the north-west corner of the Indratataka reservoir.

Central part of a lintel showing Indra on his elephant Airavata, with two simhas *disgorging* makaras *on either side, Lolei. As guardian of the east, Indra frequently appears on this side of temples.*

The remains of the north-east tower of Bakheng carved with a devata, *and behind one of the 60 small sandstone towers on the pyramid itself.*

THE FIRST ANGKOR: CAPITAL OF YASHOVARMAN I

The reader is invited to imagine what Yashodharapura, the first Angkor and capital of Yashovarman I must have looked like at its moment of glory, with its temples, palaces, houses, gardens and ponds. It was designed so as to have at its approximate centre the hill now called Phnom Bakheng, on the summit of which Yashovarman had decided to build his state temple. The capital seems to have been enclosed within a four kilometre square earth-bank, demarcating a substantial town. Subsequent Khmer kings were never to build a town of such size, with the exception of Preah Khan at Kompong Svay about which history yields so little information. In comparison with medieval France, it should be recalled that the walls of Paris built by Philippe-Auguste around 1200 enclosed a mere 273 hectares, later extended to 439 by Charles V. Or that the outer wall of Carcassonne city was no more than 1,700 metres long and enclosed an area less than one-tenth that of Yashovarman's capital!

The earth-bank of the original Yashodharapura can be traced for about eight kilometres on its south and west sides. The north of the western side was re-used as the east dike of the West Baray when it was constructed in the 11th century. On the section which remains clearly visible it can be seen that the earth-bank is flanked by another, some 300 metres away, which has given rise to the idea that the capital had originally been within a double enclosure. In fact, the second parallel earth-bank, which to its north connects with the south dike of the West Baray, can scarcely have been built before the middle of the 11th century, probably later, and possibly in order to provide a new reservoir.

No trace remains of the gate-lodges of Yashodharapura. They would have been at the end of the four great avenues, 13 metres wide and flanked with ponds, which begin from the axes of Phnom Bakheng and they may have been wooden edifices. On the other hand, it is possible as there was no stairway on the south side of the hill, that the town did not have a southward exit. By contrast there were two towards the east; one leading to the shrine on Phnom Bakheng and the other to the royal palace. In fact the causeway which began at the north-west corner of the Indratataka reservoir ended on the left bank of Siem Reap river at a point which nowadays is in the alignment of the south wall of Angkor Thom and not in that of the eastern avenue of Phnom Bakheng. The presumption is that in Yashovarman's time this causeway had been built to lead to a triumphal way ending at the royal palace, but which was subsequently completely buried under the walls of Angkor Thom. This would imply that in the first Yashodharapura there was the same arrangement of two parallel eastern access ways as would later appear at Angkor Thom; one leading to the state temple and the other to the royal palace. It is clear that subsequent remodelling over the whole area has greatly disturbed the original design, but the traces which remain allow it to be retraced without too much difficulty.

There is naturally nothing left of Yashodharapura's civic buildings, as these were in wood. No trace either of the royal palace, which to judge by the regular siting of subsequent palaces right up to the present day in Bangkok and Phnom Penh would have been north of the state temple, and consequently somewhere in the south-west quarter of what was to be Angkor Thom, the definitive capital city. As well as the palace there were undoubtedly the houses of various grandees within the city limits. One can imagine them to be on a sumptuous scale, in groves planted with trees. There would also probably have been one or more areas for less important personages. However the capital area was not entirely built up: an inscription reveals that there were paddy fields which had either been newly planted or merely kept in cultivation.

ON BAKHENG HILL: THE STATE TEMPLE

In the centre of the city was Phnom Bakheng, an oval hill some sixty metres high surmounted by the state temple. It covered most of the esplanade which the builders had boldly created by levelling the summit, though they kept the bare bones of the pyramid shape with its dressed sandstone mostly rising from the actual rock of the hill.

The base of the sacred hill was surrounded by an outer enclosure consisting of a rectangular moat 650 metres long by 436 metres wide, lined with an earth-bank which has partially survived. Brick and laterite gate-lodges rose over the cardinal points and traces of their foundations remain.

On passing through one of the gate-lodges the visitor was at the foot of a stairway cut into the rock (except from the south) and protected at the base by two magnificent stone lions, substantial parts of which have survived. It is hard to account for the missing south stairway, especially as there is a gate lodge and causeway at the bottom of the hill. Perhaps the builders ran out of time before they could insert it.

The main entrance was traditionally from the east, up the grand stairway to a wide open space traversed by a broad pathway, some 100 metres long. This large 'square' may have accommodated the temple priests' dwellings. The pathway led to the east gate-lodge of the inner enclosure which was a laterite wall 190 metres long and 120 metres wide, only traces of which remain. The oval shape of the hill accounts for the narrowness of the enclosure and for the fact that the northern and southern gate-lodges are squeezed close to the central pyramid. Like both the others, they have vanished except for their laterite bases and a few scattered bricks.

After the east entrance on either side stand the two so-called 'library' buildings with the usual west entrances, but in this case having an additional east entrance. This was probably a later addition when the temple came back into use under Jayavarman V after 968 AD. Traces of minor buildings still exist within the enclosure but there is

The eastern steps leading up to Phnom Bakheng. Lions, as was customary, guard the staircases at each level.

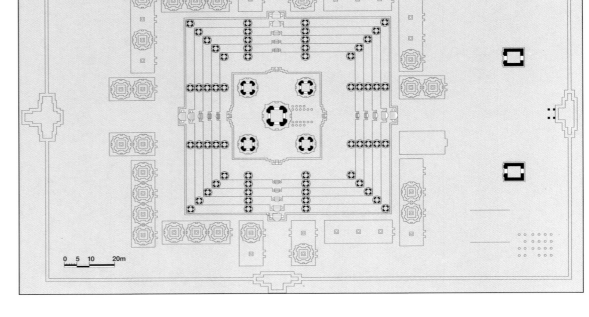

Aerial view of Phnom Bakheng. (Photo: Claude Jacques)

Plan of Phnom Bakheng showing the 108 towers that surround the central sanctuary.

no 'long gallery' like the one at Bakong. The lack of these shrines which would have housed the various guardian gods of the empire is fully compensated for by the 44 brick towers evenly spaced around the base of the pyramid. They are in groups of two, three or four, all on the same basement of dressed sandstone and they show some variation in methods of construction, using more or less sandstone, almost as if various dignitaries had co-operated with the king to bring the state temple into being. Many had a single east-facing entrance but it is likely that 18 of them had an additional western entrance, the reason for which remains obscure.

The consummate art with which the Khmers built this pyramid has long been acknowledged. The five quadrangular terraces rise above each other, decreasing in height to enhance the effect of perspective, and are breached at the cardinal points by a stairway flanked with lions which also decrease in size. The broadest terrace was 76 metres square and the topmost 47 metres square for an overall height of 13 metres. Each has a small sandstone sanctuary tower at the angles and two more which adjoin each flight of the stairways, making 12 towers in all. As the berms are narrow and each tower opens to the east, the cleric in charge of these tiny shrines on the western sides must have been slim and lithe to carry out his duties. There is one last terrace, the sixth, 31 metres square and only one metre 60 centimetres high. It is skewed westward and supports the five top towers arranged in a quincunx and open on all four sides.

The central shrine housed the *linga* of the god Yashodharesvara: 'the Lord of (the one) who bears glory', recalling the king's name, and giving the temple its name. It was probably dedicated, along with the major statues, in about 907 AD. At that time the towers were yet to be built and carved and it cannot be taken for granted that the king, who most probably died in 910, ever saw the completed state temple. With its false tiers and the surrounding towers, the central shrine must have been a splendid crown to the pyramid. It is now a mere shell, and the towers have all but vanished. Enough remains, however, for the viewer to admire the marvellous sculpture, particularly the great divinities carved in low relief on either side of the doors. The artists had continued in the Preah Ko and Bakong tradition, although not in stucco as previously but in the more recalcitrant medium of sandstone. This entailed some modification and restraint in the design details; the lintels are less exuberant, the pendants have gone, and the small figures become less numerous.

All in all, including the 44 towers surrounding the pyramid, the inner enclosure encompasses 108 towers. This is the quintessential symbolic number in the Indian universe, plus one – the central tower – which 'is' all the others, on the seven levels which have equal cosmogonic significance. Each shrine housed either a *linga* or one or more statues, and most of their pedestals have survived. They are of fine quality and the life of the temple can will be imagined, with numerous priests daily attending to the needs of each divinity.

Bakheng was abandoned after 928 AD and rehabilitated by Jayavarman V around 968, albeit briefly. Considerable efforts were made around the late 16th or early 17th centuries, when the summit towers had probably collapsed, to use the fallen blocks of sandstone to build a gigantic seated Buddha statue facing east and occupying the whole of the top terrace. The lotus cushions are recognisable but nothing more than the statue base was achieved – the Buddha's torso was never built. Due to this activity the central tower only remains as a shell, the eastern towers were almost ruined, and the western ones vanished completely.

On the summit of Phnom Bakheng the base of an enormous seated Buddha, dating from the late 16th or early 17th century, can just be discerned.

Above: Pilaster detail from Phnom Bakheng.

OTHER TEMPLES

It has long been known that there was a series of brick temples around Phnom Bakheng. They are mostly in a ruinous condition like those encircling Bakong. More than ten have been identified and some, mostly to the north of the hill, such as Prasat Bei and Prasat Bay Kaek have been partially restored.

Phimeanakas temple, erected by Suryavarman I at the exact intersection of the northern axis of Phnom Bakheng temple and the western axis of the East Baray (in no way could this have been by chance), was probably built on the site of a former shrine,

attributed to a minister of Yashovarman I. The earlier shrine was probably much smaller than the one that can be seen today and was beyond the city limits.

It is generally believed that in the Angkor region besides Phnom Bakheng, Yasovarman I also erected temples on two other hilltops: Phnom Krom which looks out over the Great Lake and Phnom Bok (not far from Phnom Kulen) where at its foot there was a town. This belief may credit the king with projects which were in fact those of some of his high officials, but the two temples do follow an identical design, with a line of three sandstone towers dedicated to Shiva, in the centre, Vishnu to the north and Brahma to the south. There is no inscription to give the date of their dedication or the name of their builder.

One thing which is absolutely certain is that many shrines vanished during the subsequent centuries, both within and without the city walls, as the Khmers repeatedly transformed the Angkorean landscape. Only painstaking excavations, which would be an immense and practically impossible undertaking, could reveal anything like the true total.

The three sandstone towers of Phnom Krom are dedicated to the three Hindu deities: Shiva in the centre, Vishnu to the north and Brahma to the south.

Above: A hamsa, *(or mythical swan), the vehicle of Brahma decorates the base of the pedestal in the shrine dedicated to this god on Phnom Krom.*

Right: Plan of Phnom Krom.

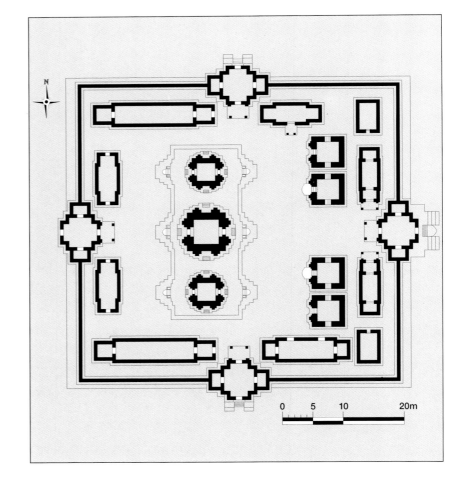

0   5   10   20m

THE EAST BARAY

Yashovarman was not content with building an immense capital – he still needed to ensure his prosperity, a king's prime duty, and this entailed securing a regular water supply. Accordingly, and probably at the start of his reign he ordered the construction of a gigantic *baray*, more than eight times the size of the one built by Indravarman I. Now named the East Baray, it was first named after the king and his capital: Yashodharatataka, 'the reservoir of Yashodhara'. It was about seven and a half kilometres long and one kilometre 830 metres wide and could store approximately 55 million cubic metres of water when the depth was four or five metres. To 'bless' this reservoir the king raised a great stele at each corner engraved with four long Sanskrit poems placing it under the protection of the goddess Ganga: 'the Ganges'.

The supply to the *baray* came mainly from a canal running some two kilometres from the Roluos river and leading to a point near the north-east corner where the dike is somewhat lower. Rainwater and maybe also spring water inside the *baray* would have supplemented the supply. There are indications too that there could have been a sluice-gate system at the south-west corner which is the least elevated, and that from there a network of culverts channelled water to paddy fields and groves of fruit trees. It is estimated that eight thousand hectares of paddy field could have received supplementary irrigation in this way. A recent hypothesis claims that there was in fact no system to run off the water and that the reservoir was solely for religious ritual, or to provide drinking water or even for aesthetic enjoyment. It would be puzzling however if such an immense undertaking was needed just for this, and why was the reservoir sited so far from the temples and the capital? The *baray* probably dried out several centuries ago and the village of Pradak, whose name ('holy water') recalls the great reservoir, now stands there.

After the grand *baray* was completed, Yashovarman installed some 450 metres south of it a group of four major *ashramas* where 'ascetics' versed in the lore of the main religious sects of the empire could be lodged. The only evidence for their existence are three sheltered stelae carved by devotees of Brahma, Vishnu and Buddha. Conspicuous by his absence is Shiva – the most important of the gods then worshipped in Cambodia. The elementary principles of symmetry indicate that his *ashrama*, which undoubtedly existed, was sited precisely where Pre Rup temple, built over it some sixty years later, now stands. The stelae also mention that the abbots of the *ashramas* were the joint managers of the *baray*. So far, the temples and major works have been described but not the men who brought them into being. A large workforce must nevertheless have been required to create this almost superhuman group of projects in a 20-year period. Clearly, more research into the extent and purpose of the hydrological works in the Angkor region needs to be carried out.

An acroter, or miniature building, on a corner of one of the towers of Phnom Krom.

The East Baray dried up many centuries ago and has been transformed into fields.

Opposite: The brick prasat *of Baksei Chamkrong was built on top of a laterite three-stepped pyramid.*

An example is the East Baray, which, as mentioned above, is seven and a half kilometres long and one kilometre 800 metres wide. Its dikes, which are today somewhat variable in section and were higher on the south side than on the north, have an estimated volume of approximately eight million cubic metres of displaced earth, excavated most probably from within the *baray* itself and from the perimeter canals. A contemporary comparison might be a motorway which requires the excavation of 100,000 to 150,000 cubic metres of earth for each kilometre, some three times less than for the *baray*.

George Groslier, the archaeologist, set out to calculate the time it took to build the great 12th century temple of Banteay Chhmar and showed by experiment that a workman could carry about two cubic metres of rubble per day for a distance of 30 metres. On this basis it can be reckoned that about six million man-days were needed for the embankment alone of the East Baray. Calculating a reasonable number of workmen at four thousand, if the other great projects proceeding simultaneously are taken into account, the work would have been completed in a thousand days, or three years, assuming they worked continuously and had no stoppages due to bad weather.

It is evident first of all that as the *baray* was begun in 889 AD it could not have been completed in such circumstances before 892, and probably took somewhat longer, and secondly an appropriate number of skilled workers should be added to this hypothetical workforce of 4,000.

Furthermore, to gain an idea of the overall size of population able to provide and sustain such a workforce it would need to be multiplied by at least five, and probably by six, seven or more. It is unlikely that the Angkor region could by itself have provided so many workmen, so major population movements could well have been required, probably from conquered lands, according to a system described formerly by the Chinese and sadly often practised in South-East Asia since then, as recorded in the Royal Chronicles.

Besides, the East Baray is far from having been Yashovarman's sole project. To mention only the major works, there was the capital city with its 16 kilometres of enclosure wall and, at its centre, the state temple with the preliminary levelling of the hilltop. The architect Jacques Dumarcay has estimated furthermore that the monument of Phnom Bakheng was made with about eight and a half million cubic metres of sandstone, to which must be added some four and a half million bricks. Add to this the dike-causeway which linked this complex with the Lolei *baray*, more than ten kilometres away, the enclosure of the north part of the *baray*, and innumerable kilometres of culverts. These few facts, by no means the whole story, will suffice to give some inkling of the fantastic achievement represented by King Yashovarman's capital. There remains the possibility that the sum total of these achievement may be erroneously attributed to Yashovarman, leaving no role in them for his sons.

THE HERITAGE OF YASHOVARMAN

It was one of Yashovarman's sons, Harshavarman I, who succeeded to the throne, as far as is known, uneventfully. His reign lasted more than ten years, although its exact duration is unknown. From the evidence of the inscriptions he seems to have had neither the energy nor the effulgence of his father and it is likely that his actual power was less in evidence.

Nevertheless he is credited with the admirably proportioned pyramid of Baksei Chamkrong, a laterite building within the north-east corner of the outer enclosure of Phnom Bakheng itself. This is the only pyramid which was not the focal point of a state temple and it is capped by a substantial brick tower housing the statues of Shiva and his spouse Devi, dedicated to the memory of Harshavarman's parents. Thus the temple had an analogous role to those of Preah Ko and Lolei. It may be that when Angkor was abandoned after 928 AD for about 15 years, the tower became

Prasat Neang Khmau, near Ta Keo town, is similar to Prasat Kravan.

dilapidated, or its decoration may not have been completed. What is certain is that Rajendravarman had it decorated, and dedicated new statues there in 948.

It was during his reign in about 920 that a group of high officials built Prasat Kravan temple east of the capital, and also its twin, Prasat Neang Khmau ('the temple of the black Lady') a great distance away, near present-day Ta Keo town, south of Phnom Penh. The splendid brick reliefs on Vishnuite themes in two of the Prasat Kravan shrines have the same subjects as the painted frescoes on the inner walls of Prasat Neang Khmau, which are much dilapidated but are the only ones to survive from ancient times. The only other known low reliefs in brick are much rougher and are in another monument of similar date: Phnom Trop in Kompong Cham province, not far from the overflow channel of the Tonlé Sap. Almost everywhere else, and then only on the outer face of the walls, the Khmer artists confined themselves to sketching the relief onto the brick and leave the finishing to be carried out in stucco as at Preah Ko.

Harshavarman's brother succeeded him in about 923 as Ishanavarman II. Despite his title of *chakravartin* ('universal sovereign') it appears that he in turn experienced a weakening of control over the empire. He died in 928 or a little earlier. There is no evidence of any temple built by him.

Opposite: Attendant of Lakshmi in brick bas-relief, northern tower, Prasat Kravan.

Below: The brick towers of Prasat Kravan were restored in the 1960s.

Chapter four
MOVING THE CAPITAL

On the death of Ishanavarman II around 928 AD, the throne passed to a king, Jayavarman IV, who probably had until then been his vassal and had, since 921 at the latest, reigned at Koh Ker, the capital of a small kingdom some 100 kilometres north-east of Angkor. It is not known how the succession came about but Jayavarman IV was an uncle by marriage of the preceding kings, Harshavarman I and his brother Ishanavarman II, and his chief queen was Jayadevi, a younger sister of Yashovarman I. This was certainly not cause enough to prove his right to the supreme throne of the Khmers. He was probably in his prime in 921 and was manifestly rich and powerful enough to have built the fine and spacious brick buildings of Prasat Thom at Koh Ker, where he had no doubt also begun, perhaps even a few years earlier, to lay out his capital city.

JAYAVARMAN IV AND HIS PROVINCIAL CAPITAL KOH KER

For whatever reason in 928 AD Jayavarman IV decided to neglect the capital Angkor and reside in his own, where he carried on with his major building programme, notably the construction of an imposing state temple. The proliferation of smaller temples in an area of some 35 square kilometres, is additional proof of the capital's wealth, built in what was after all a brief 20 or so years from 921 AD. Today it has become, or perhaps has reverted to being, one of the poorest regions in Cambodia.

It was this king who in the Angkor tradition built the Rahal *baray*, of seemingly modest dimensions (1,200 metres long by 560 wide) compared with Yashodharatataka at Angkor or even Indratataka, but undoubtedly far more difficult to engineer. The topography obliged the builders to dig part of it from solid rock and to make it follow

Statue of Brahma in the Koh Ker style, mid-10th century. It was found in the grounds of Wat Baset, Battambang. (Musée Guimet)

Opposite: Towers and pyramid of Pre Rup.

an unusual almost north-south orientation. The remains of a laterite sluice to tap its waters are still visible, but the reservoir could scarcely have been the sole source of the sudden plenty which is attested at Koh Ker and there is reason to believe – there is indeed evidence – that the great and good of Angkor had moved to the new capital to attend the new supreme king and brought their wealth and perhaps their servants and their slaves with them.

For this state temple Jayavarman IV erected a seven-storey sandstone pyramid with an overall height of 35 metres. Today it is quite dilapidated. In profile it is almost an equilateral triangle, 62 metres square at the base with the uppermost storey some 12 metres on a side. A distinguishing feature is that there is only one stairway, on its eastern side. The temple is an eastward extension of the temple in which the guardian gods of his kingdom were already being worshipped. It seems however that time ran out before it could be completed or even begun in the case of the central tower which should have crowned the pyramid and would have had similar proportions. At the summit there is only a huge pedestal for a *linga* of such extraordinary size that it was praised in several inscriptions. It was formerly housed in a structure which is presumed to have been in perishable materials since no trace of it has been found.

The salient characteristic of the art of Koh Ker is its use of huge blocks of stone; a striking feature both of the architecture and the sculpture. Sandstone was abundantly available over the whole area, and there was evidently far less of a problem in moving

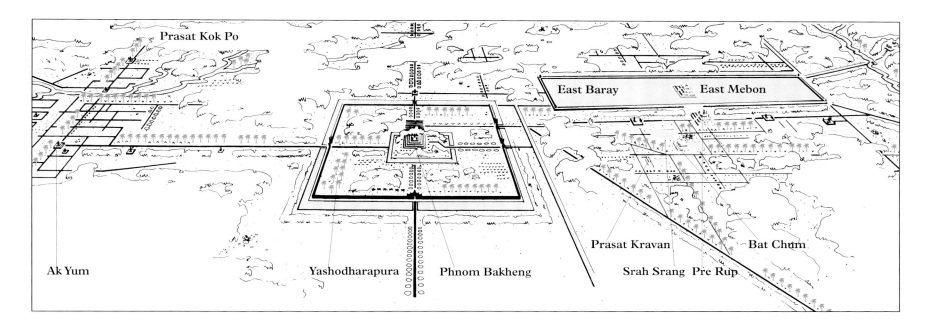

Ak Yum   Prasat Kok Po   East Baray   East Mebon   Prasat Kravan   Bat Chum   Yashodharapura   Phnom Bakheng   Srah Srang   Pre Rup

it than there was at Angkor. It is quite likely too that Jayavarman was keen to show himself able to match or even outdo the achievements of Angkor. There were, however, some major shrines built in brick, notably Prasat Kraham, 'the red shrine', which may have been reconstructed after the king had assumed the supreme throne. It was the eastern entrance pavilion and housed an immense statue of dancing Shiva with five heads and eight arms. It was sadly discovered in fragments, but enough remains to demonstrate the fine quality of its sculpture.

Jayavarman probably died in 941, which appears to be the year in which his son Harshavarman II mounted the supreme throne, or some short time before that date. The latter was not his father's designated heir, as an inscription relates that he "attained kingship with the help of a friend and that of his two arms". The friend was probably his cousin who was to become Rajendravarman, king of Bhavapura and whose mother, Mahendradevi was the sister of Harshavarman's mother, Jayadevi. An ancient lineage thus returned to the forefront, and there is no reason to doubt that it was legitimate.

The succession was, however, contested. One of Harshavarman II's generals had to wage war on the town of Indrapura, Jayavarman II's first capital, and during his short reign the king himself was embroiled in continual struggles. Only three years into his reign Harshavarman II mysteriously disappeared and there is every reason to suspect that he met a violent end. No architectural achievement is attributed to him, though it is true he had little time.

Angkor in the time of Rajendravarman.

Opposite above: Statue of Suriya from the second entrance pavilion of Koh Ker. (Photo: Claude Jacques)

The remains of Jayavarman IV's state temple at Koh Ker. (Photo: Claude Jacques)

Opposite far left: Prasat Kraham, known as the 'red shrine' from the bricks used in its construction. (Photo: Claude Jacques)

Elephant at south-east corner of the terrace of East Mebon.

RAJENDRAVARMAN: THE RETURN TO ANGKOR

It appears that until this time Bhavapura, the kernel of the ancient kingdom founded in the 6th century by Bhavarvarman I in the centre of Cambodia around Sambor Prei Kuk, had managed to keep largely independent of the 'supreme kings'. After the death of Jayavarman IV, King Rajendravarman of Bhavapura, who was possessed of considerable energy and had succeeded his father King Mahendravarman several years before, decided to help his cousin Harshavarman II mount and retain the supreme throne. He was not personally entitled to the succession but the struggle for his matrilineal ancestry incited him to seize the supreme throne on the death of his cousin in 944. The court poets emphasise that Rajendravarman was 'greater' than his predecessor "in age and in the accumulation of his virtues". In the inscriptions such a derogatory comparison is extremely rare, to the point that it has been taken as Rajendravarman's self-justification for taking over power after his cousin.

Although they were unrelated, Rajendravarman was a great admirer of Yashovarman I and he returned to the site of Angkor to re-establish the capital of the Khmer empire. It is probable that he initially established himself in the former royal palace. His first major work of piety was to restore the nearby temple of Baksei Chamkrong which had in all likelihood fallen into temporary disuse during the Koh Ker interlude. Rajendravarman "added a splendid stucco decoration" (which has now vanished) to the tower which had been built by Harshavarman I. The shrine's new god was dedicated on Wednesday 23 February 948, to be precise, at 9.40 am. It was a 'gold' statue of Paramesvara and not a *linga* as might be expected when this name for Shiva is invoked. The founder seems to have chosen it to echo the posthumous name (Paramesvara) of King Jayavarman II. From then on the temple was also the seat of the 'spirits' of all previous Khmer kings who are invoked in a splendid inscription which covers the whole of the tower's gate-jambs. Thanks to this inscription we have a clue as to how the Khmers would rewrite their own history at that time. They begin, as do many other traditions, by extolling various quite legendary kings and this is when the name of the *rishi* Kambu, ancestor of the Kambuja ('born of Kambu') first occurs. This name arises from a separate legend from that of Kaundinya, and nothing more is known of it.

KINGDOMS REDUCED TO PROVINCES

Rajendravarman did indeed need the protection of all the former kings. He was considered an intruder and was evidently unwelcome from the outset. Throughout his reign he had to face numerous rebellions from Khmer chieftains. His first task was to bring back under his sway the kingdoms which had become detached from the empire during previous reigns. It may have been due to the hardships he encountered in attempting this reordering that he apparently took the drastic step of simply relegating the kingdoms to the status of *vishaya* or 'provinces'. It is a safe bet that this radical reform was deeply resented by his former equals, the ousted kings.

Rajendravarman also waged war beyond the empire's frontiers. At one point – the date is not known – he sent a force on an expedition in which "the town of the king of Champa, which has the ocean as its deep moat, was reduced to ashes by warriors who obeyed his orders." The information is very imprecise as Cham towns were all near the sea, but it is evident nevertheless that the king was powerful enough to venture a long way from his home base. The reason for the expedition is obscure but the impression is that for long periods the Chams and the Khmers would raid each other and then seek revenge, without its being clear which side was the instigator.

On the Thai flank, Rajendravarman left various clues which tend to indicate that he had little difficulty in regaining all the lands which had been under the rule of Yashovarman I.

A NEW CAPITAL SOUTH OF THE EAST BARAY

Rajendravarman hastened to build a new capital in the centre of the south bank of the Baray. It could well be that he chose the site on the grounds of ease of communication across the immense reservoir, acting as a turntable. The monuments of his reign, as might be expected, are mostly grouped in this zone. As well as Pre Rup there was the East Mebon rising in the middle of the *baray* and the Buddhist temple Bat Chum, built by the kingly architect who also dug out the small *baray* of Srah Srang. The temple of Kutisvara, now in ruins can also be assigned to his reign, as can another temple which has vanished and was replaced in the 12th century by Banteay Kdei.

Of the capital founded by Rajendravarman, little more than the state temple Pre Rup, rising due south of the East Mebon, can now be seen. We know however that a laterite causeway formerly lined with boundary stones ran from the temple towards the east. Its surveyed length is more than 100 metres and unfortunately the modern road cuts through it. The city limits can no longer be discerned and its builders may well not have had time to surround it with moats. But its area can be reckoned on the

Two views of the temple of Bat Chum.

Inscription K528 on the stele of East Mebon, dated 953.

basis that Pre Rup is about 500 metres south of the south dike of the *baray* which was clearly its northern boundary. The length from north to south was thus about one kilometre, and as Khmer cities were generally square the area was about one square kilometre. The incompleteness of the city is probably due to its short life, since work ended at the death of its founder in 968 after a reign of some 20 years.

The normal rule would have been to erect Rajendravarman's royal palace north of the state temple of Pre Rup, between it and the *baray*, but to date no vestige of it has been found except perhaps for a pond with laterite facing. For its construction the king had called on Kavindrarimathana, a name (or title) meaning 'destroyer of enemies, king of poets'. He was not only an army chief and on occasion the king's 'personal envoy', but also an architect, whose name by a miracle has been preserved in the historical record. This unique circumstance is due to the fact that the architect himself bequeathed a monument which will be discussed below.

Rajendravarman also commissioned a temple in an 'island' in the centre of Yashodharatataka, to provide the finishing touch to the great *baray* of the king he so much admired. This monument is now known as the East Mebon. It sits on a solid mass of masonry 120 metres square and rises at least four metres above the bottom of the *baray*, giving the appearance nowadays of a 'temple mountain' though that was not the original aim. In former times it would have seemed much lower since the water level would most frequently have been near the four landing-stages which provided mooring at the cardinal points and easy access through the gate-lodges of the second enclosure, built of brick with tiled roofs. One may well imagine barges converging on the temple on feast days, those from the palace eclipsing the others in magnificence.

At the centre five towers in a quincunx crowned the whole group. The main divinity, Rajendresvara 'the Lord of Rajendra (varman)', was dedicated on Friday 28 January 953 at about 11 am. The inscription states that to build his temple and "by universal request" the king had called on the same Kavindrarimathana who had supervised the building of the royal palace.

The Buddhist architect was to build on his own account (or rather for the well-being of his *karma*) the small temple of Bat Chum. It is outside the capital but not far from it and consists of three brick towers surrounded by a moat and with a pond in front of them. The distinguishing feature is that each tower has an inscription from different hands praising the founder, as though there had been a competition where the winner's poems had been 'published' in this way. The temple was dedicated in 953 and the architect probably died soon afterwards.

Not far from the temple there was a pagoda inhabited by monks, and around it there was a built-up area. All this has long since disappeared but to the north we can still marvel at another personal achievement of Kavindrarimathana: the small *baray* which retains its water to this day, known as Srah Srang (the 'royal bath'). The reservoir's original dimensions were 400 by 200 *yukta* or 'fathoms', (about 700 by 350 metres) and it was enclosed by the standard earth-dikes. The Bat Chum inscriptions prescribe that it should be well maintained. They state: "in this *baray* where water has been stored for the benefit of all creatures, no-one should ever bring herds of tamed elephants which would destroy the dikes!" Furthermore "in this *baray* whose waters are cooled by the trees growing on its dikes, elephants should not be allowed to bathe. If anyone tries to do this the compassionate should oppose them!" Srah Srang was remodelled two centuries later by King Jayavarman VII who added a landing-stage and faced its banks with sandstone, shortening it somewhat in the process.

The whole quarter was quite thickly populated. Kavindrarimathana had built another Buddhist shrine in the vicinity, and to the north-west of Srah Srang a high official had built the Hindu temple known as Kutisvara. Ever since the reign of Yashovarman I there had been another Hindu temple to the west of the same *baray* where the temple of Banteay Kdei, built two centuries later, now stands.

It is also probable that in Rajendravarman's reign the former course of the Siem Reap river was diverted some ten kilometres north of the East Baray to feed into a canal through a system of sluices. Much later, it seems, the canal became the main course of the river. There are still some blocks of laterite at the spot marking the intake of water, the only evidence left of the former sluice gates, and a small shrine which does not seem to figure in the index of monuments. The canal apparently joined up with another sharply winding river whose former course can be traced across and beyond the East Baray, and may certainly have improved crop productivity over a wide area.

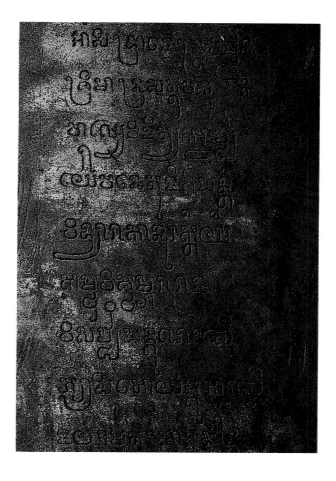

Inscription K267 from the southern door jamb of the central tower of Bat Chum, dated 953.

Left: Elephant from the south-east corner, inner enclosure, of the East Mebon.

Right: Aerial view of East Mebon and East Baray. In the background can be seen Phnom Bok from where the statues on page 25 were found.

Below: Plan of East Mebon.

Opposite: The towers and pyramid of East Mebon.

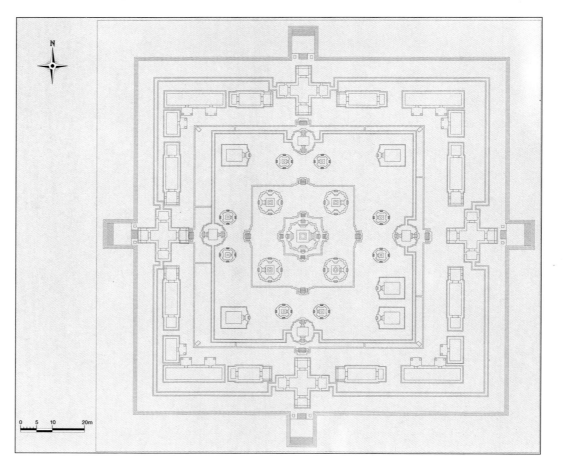

Aerial view of Pre Rup. (Photo: Claude Jacques)

THE TEMPLE OF PRE RUP

The architect Kavindrarimathana had probably already died when the state temple Pre Rup was dedicated in 961. But he could well have sketched out its first design, unless one of his disciples did so, since the concept is so similar to that of the East Mebon.

The spot on which a temple is built is always carefully determined by experts and in this case an extra reason for the chosen place was to ensure that its symmetry would point to the Shivaite *ashrama,* established by Yashovarman, south of the *baray,* along with those of the other three sects. Although the *ashrama* has not been found, there is a shelter similar to those which housed the steles of the other foundations.

Pre Rup translates as 'turning the body' and is a name for one of the rites conducted at a cremation. It was adopted because of the large so-called 'cistern' east of the pyramid where legend has it that the solemn incineration took place of the king accidentally killed by 'the gardener of the sweet cucumbers'. It is evident that, as often happens, this name has no link with historical reality. The original name would have been that of the main image, Rajendra-bhadresvara, made up of the name of the king's beloved deity, Bhadresvara, and part of his own name as a prefix.

As it was the centre of a city which should normally have had moats, the temple had none of its own. Instead, it was enclosed within two successive surrounding walls each of which was the boundary of a platform, as at the East Mebon. The platforms measure respectively 127 metres east to west by 117 north to south, and 87 by 77 metres. In its original state the area between the two walls was completely bare of shrines, or at least of shrines in durable materials, and it is reasonable to think that it was used for the dwellings of the priests who ministered to the gods.

Through both enclosure walls there are four entrance pavilions, one for each cardinal point, and all with three passageways. In the pavilions of the first wall the middle passageway has a chamber on either side evidently to house a guardian divinity.

The entry pavilions of the inner wall are simpler and open on to the pyramid, which has various buildings around it. To the east the two usual 'libraries' can be seen. Between them is the 'cistern' which provided the name by which the temple is now known. In fact it is the remains of a Nandi statue base, in exactly the right position east of the central shrine, and the fact that no trace of the statue itself has been found might indicate that it was made of bronze.

All along the inner wall there are eight 'long galleries' with tiled roofs, two for each quadrant. They have varying ground-plans; no convincing explanation for this has been advanced but they certainly housed statues. Each is made up of three differently sized sections, a very long hall opening on to a small room on either side, with entrances from the north and the south. The 'long halls' would cease to be a feature of subsequent state temples, from Ta Keo onwards, as 'peripheral galleries' were substituted for them. On the north side the 'long hall' is shorter than the others on its easterly side, as it is preceded by a small chamber which until recently housed the great stele found on the site, although it could not have been placed there during King Rajendravarman's lifetime, and followed by a shelter which may have contained the stele of the former *ashrama*.

Central tower of Pre Rup.

The plan of Pre Rup showing the towers arranged in a quincunx.

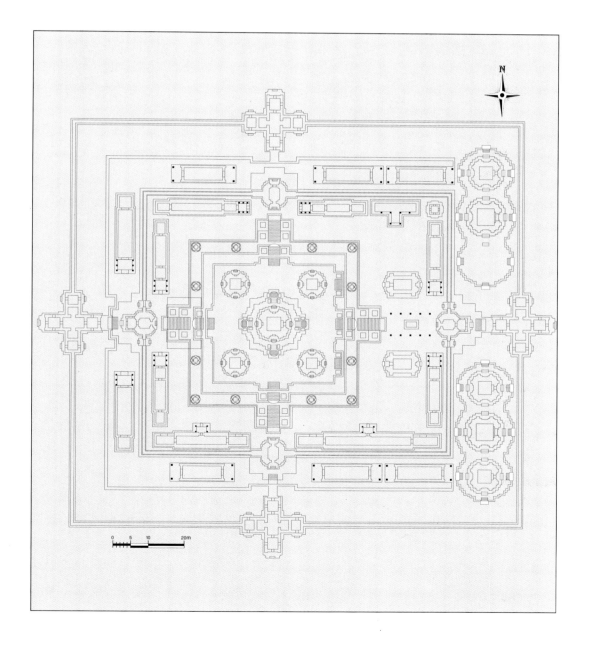

The three-tiered pyramid is in laterite and on a square ground plan 50 metres on one side at the base, tapering to 35 metres square at the top which is 12 metres above ground level, so it is very steep. The first level has 12 small brick tower-shrines so close to the wall of the next level that it is hard to squeeze into two of the ones on the west side. On the second level there is nothing save for two stairways to the east, somewhat strangely placed in alignment with the towers of the summit, but only there for aesthetic reasons as they are practically unscalable.

At the top there are four tall towers at the angles. They housed statues of Shiva to the north-east and Vishnu to the south-east, and behind them to the west their consorts Gauri and Lakshmi. The towers were built of brick and coated with a lime mortar which has now vanished except for part of the south-west tower where there are still vestiges of female guardians, in particular a four-headed Brahmi to the north on the east side and a Varahi with a boar's face, corresponding to Vishnu's boar avatar, to the west on the south side. Finally, the central tower rises on a two-stepped pedestal.

The main divinities of Pre Rup temple were dedicated in 961 or early 962 AD, some eight years after those of the East Mebon and an even longer interval separates them from the completion date of Rajendravarman's new palace. Clearly the construction period was protracted, especially as this temple is smaller than those of previous kings.

It was definitely after Rajendravarman's death and probably in the reign of his son Jayavarman V that the buildings between the outer and inner walls were introduced, as well as the new long buildings all on the same basement to the south, west and east, and most prominently the massive brick towers which fit clumsily into the east side in groups of three. Probably none of these buildings was actually completed. One of the great eastern towers in particular hardly rises above ground level, while the carving of the lintels on the other towers reflect unfinished work at every stage.

It is probable that the temple was hastily deserted in the reign of Jayavarman V, but curiously on the south pier of the upper north-east tower door there is an inscription from the reign of Jayavarman VI (end of 11th or beginning of 12th century) which is in fact the only evidence at Angkor for that particular king.

Below: The central sanctuary of Pre Rup from the east.

Opposite above: Stucco bas-relief of a devata *from the south-west tower of Pre Rup.*

Opposite below: Lintel with Indra on a single-headed Airavata.

BANTEAY SREI

Towards the end of Rajendravarman's reign the name appears of a man who seems to have been one of his most faithful counsellors, the wise *guru* of the future Jayavarman V, Yajnyavaraha, who was actually a grandson of King Harshavarman I. The king granted him various plots of land, one of which was by the bank of the Siem Reap river some twenty kilometres north-east of the capital, not far from the foot of Phnom Kulen. He established a settlement there and with his brother commissioned the building of Banteay Srei temple, renowned not only for its beauty but for the rather over-enthusiastic attention paid to its sculptures by André Malraux.

Is there a link between this choice of site and the hydraulic engineering of Rajendravarman when he diverted the course of the Siem Reap river? It is not beyond the bounds of possibility, although the temple is some distance upstream about eight kilometres away.

The name Banteay Srei is of recent origin and means 'the citadel of women' probably on account of its small scale. The middle part of the temple seems indeed to have been built more for children than for adults. The door of the central shrine is scarcely 108 cm high and while it is true that the entrance pavilion of the innermost enclosure has the usual chambers for guardian divinities on either side, they are only 30 cm wide and are thus quasi-artificial. The small city which surrounded the temple was called Isvarapura. Banteay Srei occupied the standard position at the centre of a

Yaksha *guardian figure from Banteay Srei.*

Right: The plan of the town of Banteay Srei.

Opposite: The inner enclosure of Banteay Srei, from the north-east corner of the second enclosure.

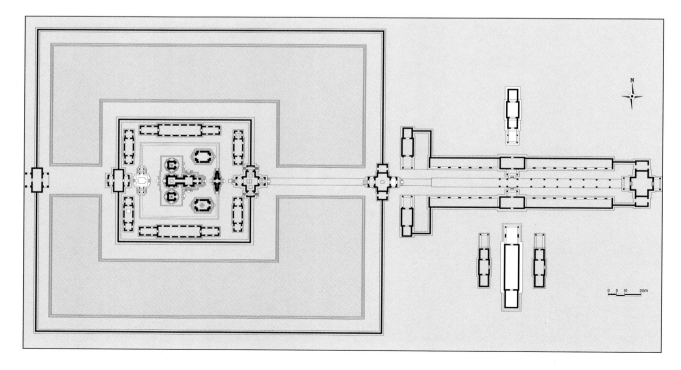

Guardian from the south side of the central tower.

Above right: Aerial view of Banteay Srei.

Opposite: Indra on three-headed Airavata from the east pediment above the entrance to the central sanctuary.

small settlement, with in this case only its eastern boundary marked by the so-called 'entrance pavilion number four', some 150 metres from the central shrine. To the south the Siem Reap river meanders considerably and therefore fails to correspond to the traditional boundary of a Khmer city. There does not seem to have been the usual earth-bank enclosure which has given rise to the supposition that the town, which might have been 300 metres square, was enclosed within a wooden palisade, although no trace of such an enclosure has been found to date.

The outer entrance pavilion, in the temple's characteristic pink sandstone, is quite spacious and has projecting deep porches to the east and the west. This broad entrance is flanked by two much smaller ones whose function is unclear. From the pavilion onwards, the high quality of the sculpture is striking. It leads on to a paved causeway some 70 metres long (running east to west) bordered by boundary stones and flanked by galleries with a plain laterite wall as their outer face, the inner face being a line of pillars. Around the mid-point of this corridor are two chambers, each with porches forming an exit to the north and south respectively. The north-facing chamber leads to a 'long hall' with a northern porch, while the south one leads to three parallel 'long halls'. The significance of the architectural layout of these four laterite shrines remains as mysterious as their function. All these buildings originally had tiled roofs. The corridor widens out as it approaches the main shrine into two small 'elongated halls'. It is clear that at this place the architect intended to enclose a sacred area accessible both from the causeway and from the town.

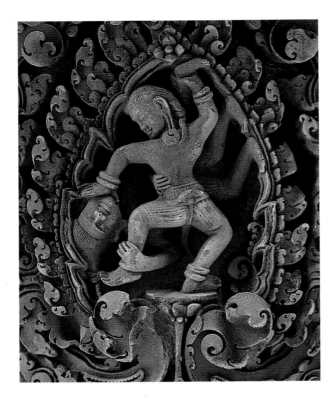

Details from lintels
Above: Krishna killing a demon, from the south lintel of the north sanctuary.

Opposite: The duel between Valin and Sugriva from the north lintel of the central sanctuary.

The temple itself is surrounded by three enclosures each with entrance pavilions to the east and west. In metres they measure respectively 95 x 110, 38 x 42 and 24 x 24. The space between the second and third enclosures is almost all taken up by a tank-moat faced with laterite steps and broader to the east than to the other cardinal points. It is crossed by a causeway to the east and to the west, so there was no plan, as there was for example at Bakong, to build the dwellings of the temple priests there.

Between the second and first enclosures there were 'long halls', two to the east and west and one each to the north and south. They were in laterite with tiled roofs and are today in a rather dilapidated state.

The first enclosure surrounds a single group of buildings consisting of three sanctuary towers on the same T-shaped terrace. In front of the central shrine there is an anterior chamber, flanked by two 'libraries'. The enclosure opens to the east through the small entrance pavilion described above, while to the west the pavilion is replaced by a shrine which contained a fine statue of Shiva with his spouse Uma sitting on his left thigh, now an exhibit in the Phnom Penh National Museum. On this side, only two small passageways provide an exit from the enclosure. The top of each of the six stairways of the central terrace was protected by two guardian figures, monsters with human bodies but different heads, kneeling on one knee. Four types of head have been retrieved: monkey, lion, *garuda*, and *yaksha*. In the central shrine was housed a Shiva *linga*, worshipped under the name of Tribhuvanamahesvara and gave its name to the whole temple 'the great Lord of the threefold world'. The north sanctuary, preceded by *garuda* guardians, housed the god Vishnu. His statue was donated by a relative of the founder and has survived. The south shrine, preceded by lion guardians, certainly contained another Shiva *linga*, donated incidentally by the founder's younger sister, but the lion guardians could indicate that there was also a statue of Devi, Shiva's other spouse, perhaps in her terrible form of Durga.

This summary description of the monument has omitted the renowned splendour of its decoration. On the three main towers and the front chamber not an inch of stone has been left uncarved. The lintels and the male and female guardian figures arouse special admiration. And it is at Banteay Srei that the carved pediments, remarkable in every way, make their first appearance, particularly those of the 'libraries' with their marvellous sequences from the Hindu legends.

The temple was particularly long-lived. We know from an inscription that King Srindravarman published an order in its favour on Thursday 4 July 1306 and from that it is clear that the founder's line of descent had not become extinct by that date. Rajendravarman was still alive to see the dedication of the central divinity of this charming monument on 22 April 967. It is probable however that he never saw it completed, as he was to die at the beginning of the following year, most probably

Moving the Capital   109

East pediment from the north 'library', showing an episode from the Mahabharata *in which
Indra attempts to put out a fire in the Khadava forest by sending rain.
However Krishna's arrows prevent the water reaching the ground.*

*East pediment from the south 'library' showing Ravana shaking
Kailasa Mountain in order to disturb the meditating Shiva.*

Right: Vishnu in his incarnation as a horse, Hiyagriva, is clutching the heads of the demons, Madhu and Kaitabha, whom he has just slain. West lintel of the inner entrance pavilion.

Below: Vishnu in his incarnation as a nara simha *holds the king of the asuras, Hiranyakasipu, upside down and rips his chest apart. From the northern long gallery on the north side of the third enclosure.*

Opposite: West lintel from the central sanctuary showing the moment from the Ramayana *when the demon Ravana makes off with Sita, Rama's wife.*

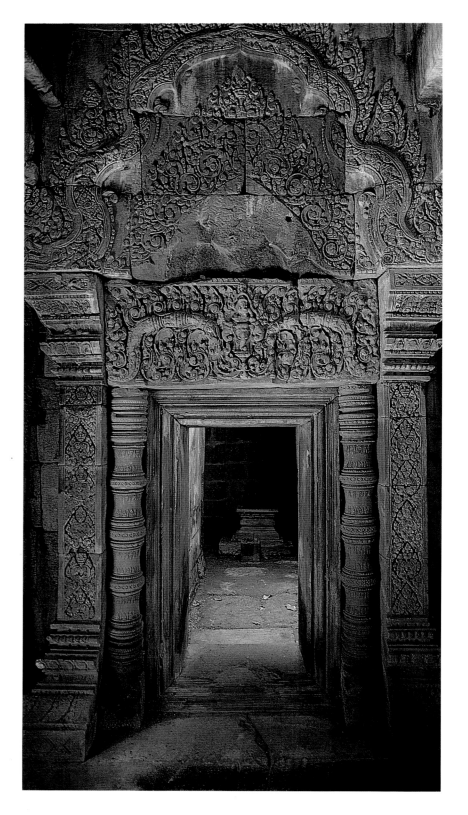

One of the devatas *from the southern tower of Banteay Srei. Unlike the later* apsaras *of Angkor Wat she is looking down.*

Right: Unfinished pediment above the east door of the central shrine.

Opposite: The innermost east entrance pavilion, now isolated since the collapse of the wall of the inner enclosure.

Statue of the bull Nandi, Ta Keo.

Opposite: The sandstone towers on the top level of the steep temple mountain of Ta Keo remain uncarved.

through a palace revolution. There is reason to believe that the fine palace built by Kavindrarimathana north of Pre Rup was destroyed during the revolt.

JAYENDRANAGARI, 'THE CAPITAL OF THE VICTORIOUS KING'

Rajendravarman's son was to take his place under the name of Jayavarman V. He evidently set to work quickly. On 3 July 968 he signed a decree granting privileges to the temple of Banteay Srei and to other foundations of Yajnyavaraha, his *guru*. Another decree of the same year related to the old temple of Phnom Bakheng which would indicate that he had re-occupied the palace of Yashovarman I.

Such administrative activity should not obscure the fact that he had to struggle hard to impose his rule: "During the great combat to possess the land, as they were suddenly faced with death raining from the countenance of this powerful king (...), the bravest enemies to the last man fled in terror and abandoned their presumptuous folly." The battles doubtless lasted many months, as it is quite probable that the royal consecration which marked the end of the crisis did not take place before 970.

Some years after Jayavarman V assumed power, the old capital of Yashovarman I and his old palace were for whatever reason deemed inappropriate and he decided to create a new capital. He probably wished to choose a site which would be more effectively defended than those of his father or of Yashovarman I, even though it would not follow their regular plan with the state temple in the town centre. He lived on the edge of the East Baray and installed his capital on its western bank, giving it the special name of Jayendranagari, 'the capital of the victorious king', instead of the name Yashodharapura which all the other kings had adopted wherever they placed their capital in the zone of Angkor.

Work was begun around 975 AD on the temple of Ta Keo which the inscriptions call Hemasringagiri, 'the Mountain with golden peaks', meaning Meru, the centre of the world. At the same time work was begun on the palace, situated as was the rule to the north of the temple. Nothing remains of it except the sandstone landing stage built at the exact centre of the west bank of the *baray*, but extensive earthworks are also apparent in this area.

Window balusters at Ta Keo, characteristically turned in imitation of wood.

THE TEMPLE OF TA KEO

The temple of Ta Keo is the most incomplete of all the 'temple mountains'. There was scarcely time to begin carving even a few of the stones, which in this case are particularly massive. Although the small amount of sculpture which exists is of the best quality and thus the finished monument would have been magnificent, its raw state in itself makes a particularly strong visual impact.

It was connected to the east with the East Baray by a causeway lined with boundary stones and ending in a small terraced landing stage. At ground level it is a quadrilateral of 122 metres by 106 and the whole group including two ponds to the east was surrounded by moats, probably because there were none around the irregularly-shaped city limits themselves. The moats were 255 metres by 195 and were faced throughout with steps of sandstone and laterite.

On the second level the long halls which surrounded the pyramid at Pre Rup have here become continuous galleries. This is the great innovation of Ta Keo, accompanied by a surprising feature – there was no entrance gate to allow access, suggesting that the galleries were merely decorative. While the windows to the exterior are blind, although they have balusters, those to the interior as well as having bars are genuine windows. The galleries were roofed with overhanging brick vaults.

The pyramid is almost completely faced in sandstone and comprises three storeys, the final one subdividing into three steps, with an overall height of 21.35 metres. At ground level it is a square of about 60 metres on each side. The uppermost terrace is 46 metres by 44 and supports a quincunx of five shrines (like the five peaks of Mount Meru) with the central shrine being larger and, in line with tradition, elevated.

It is not known exactly how far the building of the temple had progressed by the time of Jayavarman's death, but it continued during the reign of his successor at Angkor, Jayaviravarman. It could well be that the different type of sandstone which was used to build the towers on the uppermost level (for which no other explanation is available) might be due, apart from the changing of kings, to a political circumstance which meant that the original quarries had become inaccessible.

Although the temple of Ta Keo was never 'completed' in the sense that it was not completely decorated, this in no way prevented it from being active for a while, at least from the time it was dedicated as the state temple – the exact date is unknown but it must have been around 1000 AD. After the violent take-over of power at Angkor by Suryavarman I, the king donated the temple and the adjacent palace to his minister Yogisvarapandita, a former minister of the preceding king, and it would not be surprising were this gift to have been a recompense for betrayal. The minister, indeed, made use only of the ground-level shrines where the inscriptions are to be found, as the rules certainly did not allow an official, however high-ranking, to have shrines on a higher level than those of the king.

Dating from later years, there is an inscription from the end of the 13th century, which dedicates a pious work to King Jayavarman VIII and bears further witness to the efforts made during his reign towards the renaissance of the Hindu temples. We do not know how Ta Keo fared during the intermediate period.

In another connection, several temples, including one near Siem Reap in the compound of Wat Preah Einkosei, were built by Divakarabhatta, a scholarly Brahmin born in India near Mathura on the banks of the river Yamuna. It is not known why he travelled to Cambodia, but he married Indralakshmi, a younger sister of Jayavarman V, even while Rajendravarman was still alive. He had been in Jayavarman's court for some time, and may have been the author of poems of exceptional quality engraved on the steles of the East Mebon and Pre Rup.

Despite its very stormy beginnings, Jayavarman V's reign seems to have become one which could be considered outstandingly peaceful: a rarity in Khmer history. Calm seems to have prevailed after his coronation both within the empire and at its borders. The king may however have campaigned to extend his father's domain in Thailand, where a considerable number of Khmer inscriptions mention him in the north-east, and as far as Nadun, some 100 kilometres north of Buriram. The inscriptions from Jayavarman V's reign often contain decrees concerning the temples of his empire and thus give details about a number of judicial matters respecting land-ownership litigation. For example there is the account contained in a Sanskrit poem of the cases brought by Sahadeva, the great-grandson of, and

Decorative carving seems only to have been begun on the base of the pyramid of Ta Keo.

Below left: The plan of Ta Keo.

Overleaf
The pyramid and towers, Ta Keo.

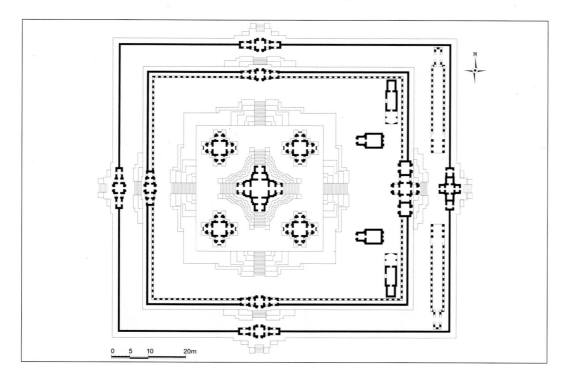

0 5 10   20m

apparently the heir to land bequeathed by, a certain Gavya, against people who had attempted to seize it and declare their ownership:

• "On the death of Gavya three men: Hi, Pu and Ke, intending to gain possession of these lands by force, declared "this land is ours."
• Hem ordered Pu to personally take away the boundary stones of the property which had been placed there by order of the king.
• Gavya's descendent, Sahadeva, informed King Jayavarman (V) in writing of the offences committed by these people.
• the act of Pu and accomplices was thoroughly investigated by ministers and court counsellors and was recognised by the king as manifestly unlawful.
• "let Hem's lips be cut off and Pu's hands be severed according to the guilt of each of them," thus was the king's order.
• and Sahadeva asked the king for Ke, the son of his maternal grandfather, who handed him over together with his family and his lands.
• later those named Pan, Ap, Gadakesa and Isanasiva as well as the woman named Ayak laid claim anew to the lands of Gavya.
• Although they had seen and heard the tale of the fate which befell those who had tried to seize those lands, they were foolish enough to want to take them. (Sahadeva complains to King Jayavarman who orders an inquiry).
• by order of the king, Ap had his feet crushed and suffered from this; Pan had his head crushed and died as a result.
• as for the woman Ayak, she had her head crushed and her relatives fled in fear headlong in all directions to hide."

The above is a sample of the punishment meted out to the foolhardy. The inscription also tell of many forms of corporal punishment; 'cageing', blows to the face, beating with sticks, cutting off ears or the nose, or for people of the highest castes, stiff fines. Capital punishment also certainly existed, but no definite example is recorded in the epigraphy.

Jayavarman V died around the year 1000 AD. A new period of dramatic upheavals was to befall the Khmer empire.

Chapter five
ANGKOR IN THE 11TH CENTURY

Immediately after the death of Jayavarman V around 1000 AD, and at the same time that his close family disappears from the Khmer historical record (none of its members are ever mentioned in subsequent inscriptions), the Khmer empire was once more plunged into great turmoil.

At first the inscriptions give the name of a king, Udayadityavarman I, crowned in 1001. His mother was the sister of one of Jayavarman V's spouses, which certainly did not of itself give her son the right to the supreme throne as some have maintained. The argument is that this woman was descended from the 'line of the kings of Sreshthapura' but this isolated reference to an ancient legend only serves to show clearly and simply that the new king had no direct link with his immediate predecessors.

His maternal uncle had been a general under Jayavarman V and it is possible that this very uncle could have helped him to mount the supreme throne, doubtless obtained through bitter conflict. There is however no trace of those who would have counted among his main adversaries: the close relations or direct descendants of Jayavarman V, of whom there must have been many.

However, as no trace remains of Udayadityavarman's presence at Angkor it is not even sure that he ever went there as king. At Koh Ker an inscription records an edict of his, dated Friday 13 February 1002. Might it have been in this former capital that he tried to make his seat in order to strengthen his challenged rule? Whatever the facts of the matter, he was to die soon after this date in unknown circumstances.

Buddha under naga *in the Bapuon style, 2nd half of the 11th century, Bayon. (Musée Guimet)*

Opposite: Battle scene from Hindu legend, entrance pavilion, Bapuon.

123

Head of Buddha, Bapuon style, 2nd half of the 11th century, from the east entrance pavilion of Ta Prohm. (Musée Guimet)

JAYAVIRAVARMAN AT ANGKOR

In fact in the same year 1002, two rival princes claimed to have been crowned 'supreme king' of the Khmers – Suryavarman I and Jayaviravarman. The latter had set up in Angkor itself, apparently in the palace of Jayavarman V, and carried on the building of Ta Keo. He was a self-styled descendant of the (legendary) 'line of Kaundinya and Soma', which once again suggests that his rights were insecurely linked to ancient legend and his accession based on violent conquest.

Jayaviravarman certainly reigned over the Angkor region as well as those of Battambang to the west and Kompong Thom to the east, where traces of his jurisdiction have survived. But his domain probably did not extend much further, although it is possible that stones engraved with this king's edicts were destroyed by his victorious successor.

In the province which is today Kompong Thom he is mentioned not far from Koh Ker, leading to the speculation that he might have been directly responsible for the disappearance of Udayadityavarman I. The last known inscription of his reign reproduces an edict issued on Saturday 25 May 1006, but all the evidence indicates that he reigned until 1010.

At Angkor itself he may have been responsible for works which have attracted too little attention until now, although their existence has been known since the 1930s. I refer to an imposing wall some ten metres high lined with a considerable embankment, which runs approximately from the north-east angle of Angkor Thom to the north-west angle of the East Baray. It is clearly a defensive wall and it should be emphasised that it is the first of this type in the region. Jayaviravarman was indeed soon threatened by Suryavarman I and it is understandable that he wished to have an effective protection for his capital. However he did not have time to complete his defensive works, and even if he had managed to do so, his rival turned out to be so much more powerful than him that the outcome would probably not have been different.

It should be noticed that the mere existence of this wall proves conclusively that the Siem Reap river at that time, and even more so at the time of Yashovarman I, did not follow the course it does today, as is customarily affirmed. In fact the river probably ran much further to the north in a bed now somewhat dislocated but still traceable throughout its length. The river's present course was then only a sector of the canal system for channelling water. The exact hydrographic history of the whole zone has however been too little studied to allow for definitive statements.

The plan of Angkor shows the wall forming an almost perfect square with the East Baray dike to the east, the present-day wall of Angkor Thom to the west and the dike-causeway leading from the *baray* to the east gate of Angkor Thom – the so-called

'Gateway of the Dead' – which had of course not yet been built. This does not imply that the causeway was not already in existence. It is not improbable that this was the enclosure of the capital designed by Jayaviravarman.

The plan also shows that subsequently the north wall was breached to allow the Siem Reap river to flow through, thus bringing it onto its present course. Nothing suggests however that the wall was breached before the 16th century.

But if the hypothesis is correct, it would indicate a state temple well away from the centre of the capital city, which is unusual. As we have seen, this was already the case when Jayavarman V initiated the temple, so Jayaviravarman had to adapt somewhat rapidly to a pre-existing state of affairs. In seeking to protect themselves more effectively, both kings could well have had to set aside to an extent the symbolic prescriptions which demanded that the state temple, representing Mount Meru – the centre of the world – be situated in the centre of the capital, itself the image of the world.

The North Khleang is earlier than the southern one. Its original purpose remains unclear.

Boundary stone in the Khleang style, c. 970, Kbal Sreay Yeay Yin near Phnom Srok. (Musée Guimet)

THE KHLEANG SANCTUARIES

Opposite the royal palace of Angkor Thom two buildings, formerly roofed with tiles, can be seen today. They are symmetrical with the triumphal way which led to the palace and the modern-day Khmers have given them the name of Prasat Khleang, meaning either 'the warehouse-temples' or 'the temples of the royal treasure'. Both their siting and their purpose are intriguing. Perhaps it should be noted at the outset that the north Prasat Khleang is earlier than its companion and their admirable symmetry was therefore not part of the original plan. Thus the positioning of the older monument cannot be explained in terms of what we now see, as it was initially some way away from a royal centre. Moreover, quite close to it and to the east, there is a small shrine in the style of Banteay Srei, which is dedicated to Vishnu and which stylistically seems a little earlier, providing good evidence that the area was built-up at that time.

The north Prasat Khleang houses several inscriptions which mention Jayaviravarman. It consists mainly of a building which is more than 40 metres long and 4.7 metres wide, open at both ends. At a later date, the large hall which it enclosed was split into two by the addition of a central tower-shaped edifice. To the east, an arrangement of peripheral galleries enclosed a courtyard. The building has very sturdy sandstone walls, 1.5 metres thick, and doubtless fulfilled a religious function, though such an unusual layout poses problems of interpretation. Whatever its original purpose, its base and walls were carved with decorative motifs of exceptional quality.

When Suryavarman I had built his palace, his architect doubtless wished to create the symmetrical counterpart of the existing Prasat Khleang to improve the perspective of the royal square. Thus the southern Prasat Khleang appeared, less carefully built than its predecessor, and in fact never completed. The two buildings have been considered sufficiently characteristic to merit a new name in the nomenclature of Khmer art styles, and the Khleang style also includes the major buildings of Ta Keo temple, the gate-lodges of the royal palace, and Phimeanakas.

Although he reigned for some ten years, Jayaviravarman does not figure in the list of great Khmer kings, at least if we go by those listed in the inscriptions. This is a wholly unusual circumstance since the Khmer kings generally did not bear a grudge towards those they had displaced. It is true however that in this case the victor, who had had himself crowned in the same year (1002 AD) as the vanquished, would certainly have found it unbearable to allow people to believe that there could have been two simultaneous 'supreme kings' in the country of the Khmers.

THE LONG REIGN OF SURYAVARMAN I

Suryavarman I, according to the inscriptions, was descended from the maternal line of Indravarman I which until then had apparently been shrouded in obscurity; his 'right to the throne' was thus in no way immediately obvious. As 'supreme King' in 1002, he was probably merely the ruler of the ancient kingdom of Sambhupura, around the site of Sambor on the Mekong, where it is likely he was crowned.

During the first decade of the eleventh century Suryavarman whittled away piecemeal the whole territory over which Jayavarman V and his predecessors had reigned. These lands were at the time under the rule of Jayaviravarman, or indeed, in the case of some, under that of an obscure princeling. The slow progress of the king can be followed as far as the temple of Bhadresvara, at the site of Wat Phu.
It is as though he had gone to seek the protection of the country's former rulers in this ancient sanctuary. From there he marched towards the west of the empire, skirting Angkor to the north and following the south route along the Dangrek ridge. In the area around Aranyaprathet, which was certainly a stronghold of Jayaviravarman, there are several accounts that he met stiff resistance. There were no doubt others. Next, Suryavarman made his painful way south to Angkor, where he at last managed to eliminate Jayaviravarman at a date which was probably not much later than 1010 AD.

It is an established fact that the final victory was long in coming. One inscription relates that Suryavarman's war lasted nine years, and while we have some evidence of his administration around today's Battambang from 1007 AD onwards, it is a fact that the first epigraphic reference to the king in the Angkor region scarcely dates back to

The Navagraha – nine deities – are traditionally equated with the celestial bodies known to the Khmers. Another interpretation is that they represent the eight directions and the zenith. (Musée Guimet)

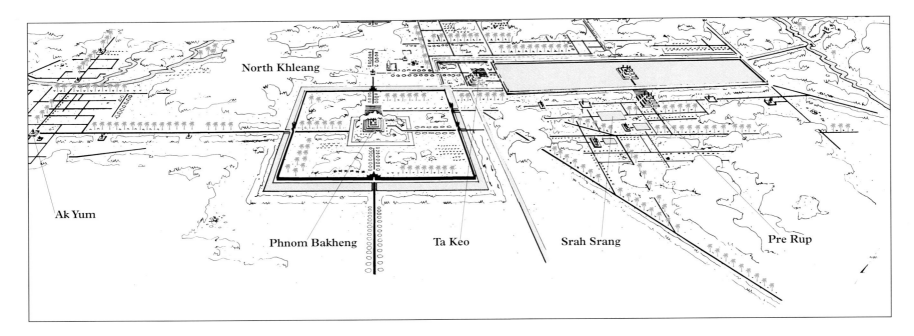

North Khleang

Ak Yum

Phnom Bakheng   Ta Keo   Srah Srang   Pre Rup

The plan of Angkor during the time of Jayavarman V.
His settlement of the area around the East Baray profoundly
changed the landscape.

Opposite: One of the so-called 'palaces' of Wat Phu, which
closely resemble the Khleang sanctuaries.

about five months before the king made all his 'functionaries' swear a famous oath. The text of this oath was subsequently carved into the walls of the east gate-lodge of his royal palace, together with the names of those who swore it: almost five hundred of these can still be read. On Sunday 9 September 1011, all these men solemnly promised:

> "We will acknowledge absolutely no other lord of the earth. We will not be enemies, we will not consort with enemies, and we will not commit perfidious acts. As to all our actions springing from our grateful love of our Lord King Suryavarman, we have a duty to perform them to the best of our strength. If there is a battle we will struggle to fight with our whole soul, we will not cling to life because of love, we will not flee when we leave the battle. In case there is no battle and we die through our own illness, we ask the gods to bestow on us the blessing of those who love their master. If our health allows us to remain long enough in the service of our master for another opportunity to die in grateful love, we must do so. If there is a royal duty whereby our Lord the King deigns to order us on a long journey to enquire about any event, we will diligently seek to enquire about the matter and will act according to our oath.

> "If it happened that we who are assembled here failed to act according to our oath, we ask our Lord the future King who is to enjoy kingship according to the *Dharma* to inflict on us 'the dread of the king' in a multitude of ways. If

we happen to betray, and fail to remain true to this act of fidelity, may he send us to be reborn in the 32 hells as long as the sun and moon remain.

"If we act in accordance with this oath, which is pure, may the King decree the protection of our pious works, of our villages and of our lands, and the support of our families for we have loved the feet of our Lord King Suryavarman who enjoys fully the august kingship according to the *Dharma* in the year 924 *saka*. As to the fruits of those who have the grateful love of their master, may they remain ours from this world to the next."

It cannot be affirmed that such a procedure had been unknown until then, but the solemnity which the king had obviously wished to confer on this ceremony was doubtless unprecedented, and it is clear that he wished thereby to ensure the unqualified allegiance of those who were in his service, and had drawn his conclusions from previous events. However, the fact that a significant number of names were struck off from various lists leads us to believe that not everyone was as faithful as he wished them to be. A curiously similar oath to the king used to be sworn annually by the whole civil service in Phnom Penh in recent times.

Although he had mastered Angkor and indubitably won great prestige, Suryavarman's troubles were by no means over. There are distinct traces of 'cleansing' in the capital, and he still had to gain the rest of the empire, especially to the south. It seems that this was not too difficult a task now that he had asserted his strength, and for a while he maintained order in the country.

One of the 65 boundary stones that line the lower causeway of Preah Vihear.

Right: Part of the inscription detailing the oath of allegiance and the names of those who partook in its swearing.

One of the seven-headed nagas *guarding the north approach to Preah Vihear.*

Left: The outermost, entrance pavilion at Preah Vihear. The temple is situated on the escarpment marking the present-day border between Thailand and Cambodia.

A portion of the Bapuon inscription giving the list of those who had sworn the oath of allegiance.

THE DEMARCATION OF THE EMPIRE: FOUR LINGA

In 1018, as though to mark out his domain, Suryavarman ordered the consecration of three *linga*, each named Suryavarmesvara, 'the Lord of Suryavarman'. One was to the north at Sikharesvara (the Lord of the Peak), nowadays Preah Vihear, a magnificent temple built on a promontory in the Dangrek mountains; the second was at Isanatirtha, an unidentified site, but *tirtha* which means 'ford' would strongly indicate somewhere on the Mekong river, to the east. Finally, the third *linga* was on the hill of Suryadri, today's Phnom Chisor, 60 kilometres south of Phnom Penh. During his conquests, Suryavarman had already placed the western *linga* at Jayakshetra, the 'field of victory', which is nowadays Wat Baset near Battambang.

He has also been credited with great conquests in lands which are in today's Thailand, as far as present-day Lopburi, where a stele has been discovered with an inscription of the king's dated 1022. The stele could however have been taken there from another site. The conquests in the Malay peninsula are more doubtful, however, and there is little hard evidence that Suryavarman's rule extended much further than the lands which had already been controlled by Jayavarman V, except perhaps in the Lopburi region.

A FORTIFIED PALACE

At Angkor Suryavarman abandoned the palace and the state temple of Jayavarman V, probably because they had been his enemy's property and therefore probably the scene of his final battle. He gave the hand of one of his daughters in marriage to his minister Yogisvarapandita, together with this whole complex. The latter was a descendant of Jayavarman II and had been in the retinue of Jayaviravarman, so little imagination is needed to suspect him of treason.

He moved closer to the original site of Angkor and built a palace which, for the first time, was enclosed by walls. This is today's royal palace of Angkor Thom, and its enclosure walls were to be used by a number of subsequent kings. There is some evidence to suggest that the palace was built over a former property belonging to the line of Suryavarman I, and that the king was doubly eager to make his seat there, because he knew he would be under the protection of his ancestors' spirits.

Within the enclosure, apart from his royal palace, about which more will become known when the current excavations are complete, he built the temple mountain which is today called Phimeanakas: 'the aerial chariot'. It is unusual because of its relatively small scale, even taking into account that its pyramid rises from ground level, and not from the usual spacious terraces. It could be surmised that, given his political situation, Suryavarman gave greater priority to ensuring his defences than to building a grandiose state temple. In comparison with other pyramid temples, Phimeanakas is smaller than Pre Rup (50 metres on one side) and Ta Keo (60 metres square) and is a rectangle of only 35 by 28 metres at its base. It rises very steeply, however, since above three laterite levels totalling twelve metres in height, the dimensions of the summit are still 30 by 23 metres.

We find here, as at Ta Keo, a continuous covered gallery which in this case allows for circumambulation, but is too cramped to house statues of the gods as it is only one metre wide. At the cardinal points it has gate-lodges with two wings and a single tower each, and at the angles the roof is slightly higher. At the centre there is scarcely the space for a single tower, built on a cruciform base two and a half metres high. This central shrine opened to the four quarters through gates which each had a projecting fore-part.

The architect of Phimeanakas re-utilised old jambs to frame the door of the central shrine, and these carried an inscription in Sanskrit and Khmer recording the merits of a minister of Yashovarman I. Even if there are indications that there were later additions to the shrine after Suryavarman's reign, the fact that these jambs were incorporated and left in this privileged position leads this author to suppose that there was a link between the minister and the king, since their siting could not have been a

Guardian lion and the very steep staircase of Phimeanakas.

Left: The plan of Phimeanakas.

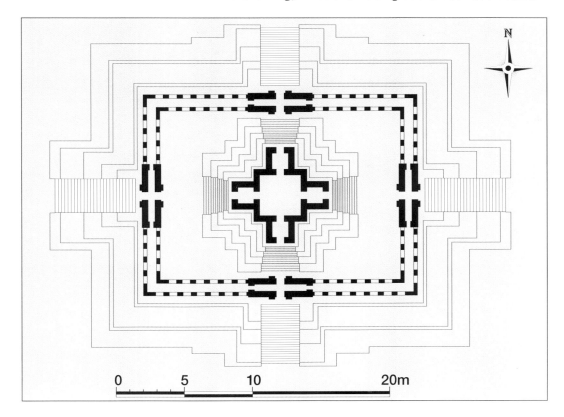

The stele of Prahal (K449), dated 1069, contains a genealogy of Khmer kings and is unusually decorated with a relief of Shiva and his consort Uma.

Opposite: The upper level of Phimeanakas, from the south-east corner of the narrow surrounding gallery.

mere chance occurrence. Moreover, the recent discovery on either side of Phimeanakas of the bases of huge wooden pillars at a level which probably corresponds to that of the tenth century, shows that there were large dwellings at this site; possibly the minister's palace.

A Wide Variety of Other Foundations

Beyond Angkor itself, Suryavarman's other foundations – or at least those dating from his reign – were considerable. To the south is the notable temple of Suryadri or Suryaparvata, 'the mountain of Surya', now called Phnom Chisor; to the north there is the aforementioned Preah Vihear temple where he revived a former religious centre which seems to have been founded by a son of Jayavarman II. From this reign (though not necessarily as direct commissions of the king) there are buildings at the great town of Preah Khan (at what is now called Kompong Svay) which is some hundred kilometres due east of Angkor. Nearer Angkor the temple of Chau Srei Vibol (also known as Prasat Wat Trach) also dates from the period.

It could well be the case that much more was achieved in this long reign of over forty years. This king, of whom so little is really known, may turn out to be one of the greatest Khmer royal builders. It was probably he, and not his successor, who carried out the construction of the second great *baray* at Angkor, now known as the West Baray. It is even more astounding than the first, with measurements of 8 kilometres in length by 2.2 in breadth. It has often been stated that this vast lake had to be created because the East Baray had completely dried out. This is a dubious assertion, since Jayavarman V had built a terrace to the east of his palace not long beforehand, and the landing stage leading to the temple of Ta Keo would also have been useless if it did not look out over the waters of the East Baray. There is also an inscription of the thirteenth century which mentions it as still functioning. Other inscriptions praise the king too for his achievements in building up the country's infrastructure. The fine road from Angkor to Preah Khan of Kompong Svay springs to mind, and there are bridges, travellers' shelters and numerous water tanks throughout his empire.

Suryavarman I was indubitably one of the great names in the civilisation of Angkor. He died in 1049 in unknown circumstances, after a reign of 47 years from his crowning in 1002.

The east entrance pavilion of Bapuon, which was completely reconstructed in the 1960s. The pyramid behind is currently undergoing restoration.

UDAYADITYAVARMAN II

The successor of Suryavarman I, Udayadityavarman II, was crowned in February or March of 1050 AD. There appears to have been no blood relationship between the two kings. On the contrary, the new ruler of the Khmer country seems to have been a relative of Viralakshmi, his predecessor's chief queen, who was descended from the line of Yashovarman I's wife, the mother of Harshavarman I and of Ishanavarman II. The reign of Udayadityavarman II was marked, however, by various upheavals, related in epic terms in an inscription which – exceptionally – celebrates his faithful general Sangrama. In 1051, at the outset of the reign, Sangrama had to crush the rebellion of a certain Aravindahrada who until then had defeated several generals sent by the king. Later, in 1065, Sangrama was once again sent out into the north-east, in a zone quite near Angkor, to put down Kamvau – a general on whom Udayadityavarman had showered honours – who had risen against the king "blinded by the effulgence of his own glory, and scheming in his heart the ruin of him to whose powerful favour he owed that glory". A short while afterwards, new troubles arose in the east, fomented by individuals whose identity is obscure. It was once more Sangrama whose task it was to counter them, and according to his eulogists he soon caught and captured them, and handed them over to the king.

It is an irresistible pleasure to quote this extremely lively account of the battle which matched the faithful Sangrama with the traitor Kamvau:

> "The glint of the scimitars, the pikes, the lances and the myriad arms which were brandished, and which rushed hither and thither made the sky shine suddenly with bright flashes.
>
> Many a brave enemy captain riddled with wounds sank into the sleep of death, with limbs stained in floods of thick blood, resembling mountain ranges.
>
> On seeing the enemy chief advance towards him with bow in hand, Sangrama, with his skilled eloquence addressed him in a proud, deep voice:
>
> 'You depraved madman, I have long sought you! How can anyone who attacks Indra not be fearful, despite being insane?
>
> Stay, stay, great hero! Show me you valour. As soon as I have the proof of it I will despatch you to the domain of Yama (the god of Hell)!'
>
> Thus challenged, the proud hero replied haughtily: 'Cease your efforts to intimidate me, o hero! Soon you will see my heroism!'

This sharp and virile arrow which I shall shoot will swiftly take you to the domain of Yama. Try, then, to ward it off with your fine words!

They exchanged these terrible words to scare each other, and vied with each other in twanging their bows, tautly strung for combat.

On his shining and strongly bent bow Kamvau had strung arrows in the image of his thoughts, and aiming at the general's jaw, shot at him.

The general, hit by these sharp arrows like a rain of flowers, was no more affected by them than the king of the mountains is by a shower of rain.

Battle scene with war elephant and soldiers, eastern outer gallery, Bayon.

Aerial view of Bapuon. (Photo: Guy Nafilyan)

Opposite above: The remains of an enormous reclining Buddha on the west side of Bapuon, built in the 16th century using stones from the pyramid.

Opposite below: Plan of Bapuon with the moat of the royal palace visible to the north.

Straightaway, with three well-feathered arrows, sounding like the humming of the shaft of Agni, he pierced his enemy at one and the same time in the head, the neck and the chest.

Torn by these sharp blows, the enemy fell to the ground with a terrible cry, as though announcing the sad news to his followers."

(Stele of Preah Ngok, side C, verses 38-49; French translation by Auguste Barth)

BAPUON TEMPLE

These disorders did not distract Udayadityavarman from his intense activity in the capital. "Seeing that at the centre of Jambudvipa there rose the golden mountain, the dwelling-place of the gods, he had a golden mountain built at the centre of his city, as though in emulation. On top of this golden mountain, in a golden temple, shining with celestial light, he erected a Shiva *linga* in gold." (trans. into the French by George Cœdès).

The reference is to the great temple of Bapuon, whose pyramid rose to the south of the royal palace and which more than two centuries later would impress the Chinese ambassador Zhou Daguan. It was certainly completed by Udayadityavarman, but it is not beyond the bounds of possibility that Suryavarman I had already conceived this grand temple and begun preparatory work on it during his reign.

In its present layout the ground plan of the temple is unusually elongated, as it is 425 metres long and only 125 wide. At first sight it is close to, and almost squeezed up against the south moat of the royal palace. Perhaps this was because the area south of the temple was a waterway which could have been a remnant of the old moats of the original Yashodharapura. Moreover, in its present state the external gate-lodge extends along the royal terraces, and there were to be later attempts to join it to these. This could not have been the intention when the temple was first built, as the terraces are of a later date. It is thus clear from the outset that the monument underwent major modifications after its initial construction. We will see that these can be attributed to the thirteenth century, and further modifications in the same period were followed by others in the 16th or 17th centuries. Nevertheless it is easy to see that in his original plan the architect was not lacking in boldness, and that he wished to achieve a more grandiose monument than had existed thereto.

Access to the temple is today via a large entrance pavilion with three passages in a cruciform plan, which has been reconstructed as far as possible with the stones found on the site. It will be noticed that none of the passages is aligned with the entrance to

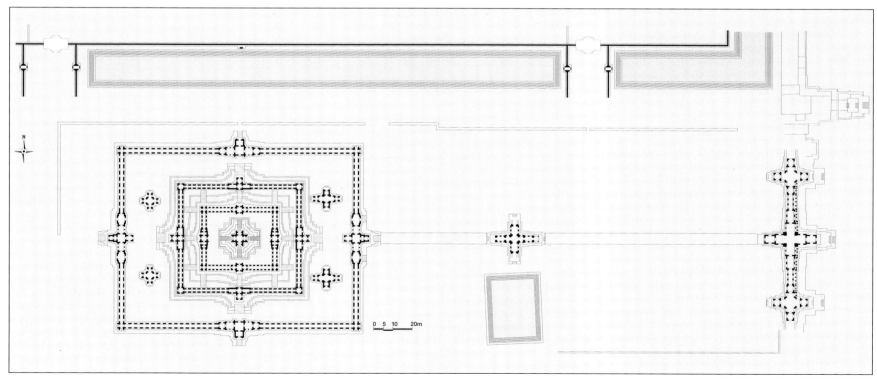

A mythological figure from the west entrance pavilion on the upper level of Bapuon pyramid.

Prasat Khleang, and that the lateral ones do not correspond to anywhere in the temple itself. The original gate lodge was probably the one which now intersects the fine sandstone causeway which runs over three ranks of round columns. The causeway is obviously a secondary addition, and runs for 117 metres initially, and then for another 55 metres to the base of the pyramid. The gate-lodge would otherwise have no reason for being where it is, and it appears that on the same level on the northern enclosure wall, which is also quite dilapidated, there are visible traces of stonework at an angle. If this were the case, it is probable that the ends of the gate lodge to the north and the south were modified by placing stairways where the walls of the enclosure began. Beginning at this second gate-lodge the overall length of the temple enclosure reduces from 410 to 238 metres which, with its breadth of 125 metres, gives more 'normal' proportions to the group. The tank faced with laterite to the south of this intermediate gate-lodge is obviously of later date, and indeed does not extend along the building.

The temple proper is a high pyramid, entirely faced in sandstone, measuring 125 metres at the base from east to west and 100 metres from north to south. Its three levels are each surrounded by continuous galleries intersected by the entrance pavilions and marked by turrets at the corners. The huge platform of the first storey, supported by a stout ornamentally moulded wall six metres high, featured to the east and the west two cruciform buildings, the eastern one being more elaborate. These occupy the same positions as the former 'libraries', but are radically dissimilar in being open to the four quarters. The eastern and western shrines were linked to each other and to the entrance pavilion by raised passageways on short columns, dating probably from the second half of the 13th century.

The second platform is supported by two tiers with an overall height of about nine metres and is surrounded by a narrower gallery than the first. The temple's entrance pavilions are all decorated with female divinities and animals but those on the second level have the additional characteristic of being profusely illustrated with charming reliefs arranged as small superposed panels which should be viewed from the bottom up, and narrate episodes from mythology and Indian legend.

The upper platform is also on a double tier of the same height as the second and it too had a continuous gallery, in this case curiously split in two by a longitudinal wall which is hard to examine as it is in ruins, but which would have supported the roof. It must have been very cramped and one writer has suggested that the gallery was a dummy or 'trompe-l'oeil' feature. A high and finely decorated base supported the central shrine which has completely disappeared. It has been assumed, without much proof, that the shrine was in perishable materials. The forthcoming investigation of the stones of the great recumbent Buddha may elucidate this question. Whatever the facts of the matter, it can be wagered that the shrine was outstandingly beautiful.

During the Hinduist revival of the second half of the 13th century the temple was probably restored and extensively modified, as mentioned in the above account, prompting the Chinese visitor, Zhou Daguan to take note, although the temple was already ancient when he travelled to Angkor, and describe it as 'the copper tower'. This gives rise to the theory that it had been – perhaps during the course of its latest renovation – sheathed in gilt bronze plaques. At a later date, as with Phnom Bakheng, the ruined stones of the temple and its central galleries were used to build an immense recumbent Buddha against the west gallery of the second level. A series of major collapses took place from 1943 onwards and the scale of work required to effect durable repair discouraged the curators until the French 'Angkor Conservancy' could at last draw on adequate technical and human support. The work began in 1958 and through the 1960s was the focus of the Conservancy's most ambitious project, aiming to reconstruct the temple using the technique of anastylosis. War frustrated the work on the project, which, however, has recently been resumed. There is reason to believe that King Udayadityavarman II also enclosed his town, and that the enclosure roughly followed that of today's Angkor Thom, being obliterated by later works.

Under his reign occurs the first mention of the *Devaraja,* the institution created two and a half centuries earlier under Jayavarman II when he was crowned 'supreme king of the Khmer kings' in 802 AD. This is because a member of the family having exclusive rights to the ritual of the *Devaraja* divinity had acceded to high rank. He was already the spouse of one of the younger sisters of Viralakshmi, Suryavarman I's chief queen, and the *guru* of Udayadityavarman II, who in gratitude conferred on him the royal title of Jayendravarman and sumptuous gifts, a list of which still exists.

The narrative reliefs of Bapuon are distinctive for being carved in a series of small panels.

The West Mebon, built on an artificial island in the West Baray. (Photo: Claude Jacques)

THE WEST MEBON

Just as Rajendravarman had built a temple (the East Mebon) on an artificial island in the centre of the *baray* which Yashovarman had created, so Udayadityavarman II ordered the building of the West Mebon in the middle of the West Baray which had been constructed during the reign of Suryavarman I. It is a most unusual monument, composed of an earth-bank which encloses a large square pond faced with steps of dressed sandstone, some 100 metres square. The dike was surmounted by a wall adorned with windows and intersected by three pavilions at regular intervals on each side.

In the centre of the pond was a sandstone platform measuring ten metres square, linked to the eastern dike by a laterite causeway. The platform was breached by a well 2.7 metres deep in carefully dressed stone, at the bottom of which a large fragment of a splendid bronze figure of recumbent Vishnu was discovered. It must have been more than four metres long, and is nowadays on view at the National Museum in Phnom Penh. It is a remarkable fact that the few large-scale Khmer bronze statues which have survived, all date from this period.

It was also in Udayadityavarman II's reign that some of the high dignitaries of the kingdom retired to hermitages on Phnom Kulen and Phnom Kbal Spean which is next to it to the west, and carved *linga* and images mainly in the Vishnuite tradition, in the stones of the river bed or nearby.

Udayadityavarman died in 1066 or shortly before, and is one of the very few Khmer kings of the Angkor period not to have received a posthumous name. Hesitations over the coronation date of his successor are a possible indication that the interregnum was troubled and that in consequence his cremation, which is the ceremony at which a posthumous name was conferred, did not take place under normal conditions.

HARSHAVARMAN III: A LITTLE-KNOWN REIGN

In 1066 or 1067 AD Harshavarman III was crowned on the throne of his younger brother Udayityavarman II, born of the same mother. He was to reign for about fourteen years. The inscriptions tell us little of his reign, perhaps because he was succeeded by a king who was descended from another line and did not wish to give him a posthumous eulogy. He probably had to face very serious internal turmoil, as had his brother, although all we know of him comes from external sources and concerns his foreign exploits.

It is known that in 1076 the Chinese emperor gave orders to the Khmers and the Chams, whom he considered as tributaries, to assist his troops as they attacked his former Vietnamese vassals at their northern frontiers, in a campaign he was planning against them. On the Chinese side, the operation was not a success; the Chams seem to have remained cautious, and it is not known to what extent the Khmers became involved, as nothing can be gleaned from the epigraphy.

The incidental alliance between Khmers and Chams was short-lived. Harivarman IV, a Cham prince who reigned from 1074-1081, boasts of a victory at Somesvara (the name of a temple which was doubtless at the centre of a city whose site is unknown) over Khmer troops commanded by a prince, Nandanavarman, who had a royal title but who has left no trace in Khmer epigraphy. He was made prisoner, and as usual, the temple was stripped of its treasures which were offered in 1080 to a Cham god, actually Ishanabhadresvara at the 'national' temple of Mi-Son.

Harshavarman III died in the same year of 1080 AD, and it is tempting to surmise that he met a violent end because of the disorders which marked his reign. It is possible that a younger brother, Nripatindravarman, attempted to ascend to the vacant throne, but he was probably not even crowned.

The Cham capital of Mi-Son is south-west of Danang.

Reclining bronze Vishnu from West Mebon. (National Museum, Phnom Penh)

Chapter six
Suryavarman II and Angkor Wat

The end of the reign of Harshavarman III saw yet another change at the summit of the Khmer empire, despite perhaps some resistance on the part of one of his brothers. At that time there appeared a king, Jayavarman VI, crowned in 1080, whom the inscriptions do not relate to any previously known royal family, which is unusual. Jayavarman VI was the son of a certain Hiranyavarman, who was perhaps a minor vassal king. He claimed to be from a 'royal family', descended from Kambu and ensconced for several generations at Mahidharapura, a kingdom or city whose exact location is unknown. A fairly likely hypothesis would place the city in today's north-east Thailand, perhaps in the region of Phimai or even at Phimai itself. Modern historians have used the name Mahidharapura to designate the new 'dynasty'. This radical change in the royal family suggests that once again the succession to the supreme throne of the Khmers did not take place without violence. It is true that the inscriptions are completely silent about the circumstances of Jayavarman's accession, but it is difficult to imagine that there was no pretender among the descendants of previous families, and that they relinquished the throne willingly.

JAYAVARMAN VI: A SIGNIFICANT REIGN, BUT WITHOUT MONUMENTS

It is probable that it was at Yashodharapura that Jayavarman VI was consecrated in 1080 by Divakarapandita, a Brahmin sage to whom he granted the title of royal *guru*. The latter bears witness to a degree of continuity since he had already been in the service of Udayadityavarman II and of Harshavarman III, and at a very advanced age, after about 50 years of service to the supreme royalty, was yet to consecrate Suryavarman II in 1113 AD. It is nevertheless a subject of some doubt as to whether

Standing bronze Buddha in Angkor Wat style from the second half of the 12th century. (Phnom Penh National Museum)

Opposite: The north-east tower and the east staircase of Angkor Wat's central massif, from the courtyard of the second level.

the new king actually kept Angkor as his capital. From this relatively long 27-year reign, there remains only one piece of written evidence, on a door jamb of Pre Rup, and, truth to tell, few epigraphic traces of the king throughout the rest of the empire. One inscription emphasises that the reign was "extremely peaceful" and one could indeed apply to Jayavarman the phrase from Carlyle's *History of the French Revolution:* "Happy the people whose annals are blank in history books!"

It is to this monarch that some writers attribute the remodelling of the third storey of Bapuon temple, at the base of the central sanctuary tower, which buried the former fine cruciform basement under a new one, just as finely constructed, but this time on a square plan. To him, also, is attributed the modification of the temple's access causeway, which was elevated between the first entrance pavilion to the east, as far as the shrine, making it into a sort of sandstone bridge resting on three lines of elegant columns which can still be admired. This would imply, significantly, that the pavilion, clearly running along the Terrace of the Elephants, was already in existence, which is by no means certain. It has been asserted above, and will be reiterated, that these modifications would, with much greater historical coherence, be compatible with the works undertaken by King Jayavarman VIII in 1243 AD.

If Jayavarman VI did reign at Angkor, it seems that he preserved the royal palace and Harshavarman III's state temple without modification. It would doubtless not have been the first time that a king descended from a new line did not build his own state temple. Before him, Jayaviravarman had preserved and continued the construction of Ta Keo, which was Jayavarman V's temple, and it is thus clear that a king did not feel obliged to build a fresh state temple if he already had a shrine which he considered appropriate. Naturally the king would have preserved the palace of his predecessors as well. This leads to the supposition that if there was a violent transition when Harshavarman III was succeeded by Jayavarman VI, Angkor was not where it took place. The current excavations at the palace should soon yield firm data on the matter. It can be seen that in our current state of knowledge, there is a large element of speculation, whether or not Jayavarman VI really resided at Angkor.

A few inscriptions after death of Jayavarman VI in around 1107, mention that he made donations for temples in various sites such as at Wat Phu, Preah Vihear or Phnom Sandak. All these are situated near the current day border of Cambodia. However, no new monument can be attributed to him, which is exceptional for such a long reign.

FAR FROM ANGKOR: THE TEMPLE OF PHIMAI

It must have been shortly before the death of Jayavarman VI, however, that the magnificent temple marking the centre of the old Khmer city of Phimai was built. Phimai has been a Thai town since the 15th century. While it is true that the Mahidharapura dynasty originated in this region, it is hard to imagine that Jayavarman VI played no role in the building of such a large monument, since the city at the time was under the rule of the king of Angkor. But there is no allusion to, or mention of Jayavarman in the inscription which gives us this information, although it is true that it was carved some years after his death.

It seems the place had long been sacred: in the temple wall, a re-utilised stone engraved with a Buddhist inscription of the 8th century has been found, together with a curious stele which has a homage to Shiva on one side, and one to the Buddha on the other. Both date from the reign of Suryavarman I. Despite appearances, can it be affirmed that Phimai temple as it exists was originally built to house the Enlightened One? While the lintels of the interior are definitely Buddhist in inspiration, the main pediments and exterior lintels are clearly Hinduist; in particular the pediment above the main entrance (which was from the south) with its magnificent dancing Shiva. It is certain, however, that in the reign of Jayavarman VII there was a Buddha statue, probably in the central sanctuary.

The lack of a major inscription is regrettable, and indeed surprising, as it would probably have resolved many of the riddles of this temple, such as the exact date of the dedication of the main divinity. On the other hand we have a date, December 1108 AD, for the erection in the south entrance pavilion of a local deity, Trailokyavijaya: 'the general of the god of Vimaya'. It should be noted in passing that the foundation of this god was due to a man who would become one of Suryavarman

The giant garuda *on the west face of the central tower at Phimai is surmounted by* Varuna, *the guardian of the west.*

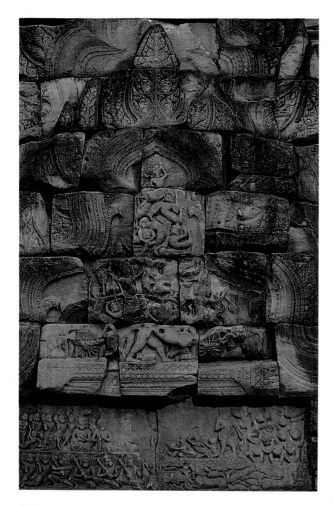

Pediment and lintel from the central sanctuary of Phimai, both showing scenes from the Ramayana.

Opposite: The west entrance of Angkor Wat.

II's great generals, and whose portrait can be seen in the 'historical' gallery of Angkor Wat. This 'god of Vimaya' – the old name for Phimai – has often been taken to indicate the name of the Buddha statue supposedly at the centre, but this is highly unlikely. He appears in fact to be the guardian of the city and apparently stood in the exact centre of the southern entrance pavilion, while the central god, whether or not he was the Buddha, would have been of Indian origin.

The peculiarity of Phimai is that it opens to the south, or more precisely to the south-south-east, which is a highly unusual orientation. Attempts have been made to justify this on the grounds of topography, or more often, on the basis that the temple is thus turned towards Angkor. To this author it would seem to require far more evidence of the links between the two cities to accept this hypothesis. A more plausible supposition is that, as the south is the direction of the ancestors, the temple housed the ancestor spirits of the line of Jayavarman VI, who would thus have been the main founder. But the absence of a stele denies us a definitive answer. Certain innovations in Phimai temple seem to have inspired subsequent architects and it is thought that in particular the main tower of the shrine, with its distinctive shape (see page 45), was the model for those at Angkor Wat.

On the death of Jayavarman VI, in 1107 or a little earlier, it was not the designated crown prince, Jayavarman's younger brother, who had died prematurely, but his elder brother who succeeded him: "Having no desire for royalty, Dharanindravarman (I), when the king, his younger brother, had returned to heaven, through sheer compassion and giving way to the prayers of the multitude of humanity deprived of their protector, governed the land with prudence." Perhaps prudently but without much firmness: it is a known fact that around that time there were two Khmer empires and probably a large number of other princedoms. Dharanindravarman I did not have time to build a single monument. Five years after his accession in a 'defenceless' capital (Angkor or elsewhere) he was overthrown 'in a one-day battle' by one of his grand-nephews, who was to reign under the name of Suryavarman II.

Suryavarman was the maternal grandson of a sister of the preceding kings, not an abnormal blood relationship in a matrilineal society. The 'norm' would nevertheless have been to await one's turn which was obviously not what the young Suryavarman II was willing to do. Once again the assumption of power was preceded by a veritable conquest of the Khmer empire which at the time was in the hands of two rulers. One of them was definitely Dharanindravarman I, but the name of the other is unknown.

After conquering Yashodharapura, Suryavarman II had himself crowned king in 1113 AD by the same Brahmin, Divakarapandita, by then doubtless extremely old, as his two predecessors and great-uncles.

For posterity, Suryavarman is above all the builder of Angkor Wat. For his contemporaries he was also a conqueror and it is indeed in this aspect that he is depicted with his generals and armies on a relief in the great temple.

ANGKOR WAT: THE CAPITAL

The eternal glory of King Suryavarman II will remain the building of Angkor Wat, literally 'the capital which is a temple', south of the former capital of Suryavarman I and his successor. Assuming that Dharanindravarman's palace was at Angkor and was the scene of the battle which caused the death of the king, it may be imagined that the area was sufficiently devastated to impel the young king to build new structures. However, it is more likely that the real reason which led the victor to build a new state temple, surrounded by a new capital, was his faith in Vishnu.

Angkor Wat was first and foremost a 'capital' as its very name recalls. It certainly included the royal palace of Suryavarman II, as it is quite obvious that the site of the former palace at Angkor Thom was too far away to be suitable. The capital was enclosed within a laterite boundary wall 1,030 metres long and 820 metres wide, giving an area of nearly 85 hectares. This was much more compact than Angkor Thom (nine square kilometres) or the first Yashodharapura (16 square kilometres) but was enough to accommodate the royal administration whose buildings have left no surface trace, as is the case in all the other locations. The terrace on which the central temple stands, in the middle of the enclosure, measures 332 x 258 metres, or less than 9 hectares: around a tenth of the total area.

Right and opposite: Angkor Wat seen from the air and from Phnom Bakheng.

The west entrance to the city from across the moat.

Left: Naga *balustrade with the towers silhouetted in the distance.*

The enclosure, beyond a berm about 40 metres wide, was surrounded by an immense moat some 190 metres broad and entirely faced in laterite and sandstone. From east to west it measures 1,500 metres and from north to south 1,300. Apart from its beauty, it simultaneously provided not only protection and symbolism, but also a reservoir with a capacity, at a depth of five metres, of around five and a half million cubic metres of water!

To enter the city, it is nowadays necessary to cross the moat on the west side over a causeway which in my view cannot, however, have been built earlier than the second half of the 13th century. We return to this matter at a later stage, but it can be argued that the moat was originally traversed via wooden bridges which may have connected with the cartways which crossed the north and south entrance pavilions. On the eastern side there is a humble earth causeway of uncertain date. There are no cartways corresponding to those at the entrance pavilions, not that this means that they did not exist, perhaps also as wooden bridges.

Four entrance pavilions provide access to the city. Those on the north, east and south sides can only be entered on foot. They are extremely well-finished buildings, with a sanctuary on either side of the entrance and are of relatively 'modest' dimensions, although each is 59 metres long.

By contrast the town's western entrance pavilion, which is the main entrance, doubtless because the great temple's principal inhabitant was the god Vishnu, is almost 230 metres long and has three pedestrian passages capped with towers (which implies that they were also shrines), and two cart-ways. From this entrance onwards, an impression of the main temple's decoration can be formed, with images of divinities – especially those within it, often termed *apsaras* – which are every bit as beautiful.

Beginning from this pavilion, there stretches a 350-metre paved causeway, elevated more than a metre above the surrounding ground level, as though it were a platform to bear the great temple, and so to demarcate the sacred enclave. It is crossed by six double porches which mark the departure points for the town's former roads, some 50 metres apart from each other. These roads crossed with others and we have certain traces of two of them, at least: those which join each of the cartways to the western stairways of the platform. On this basis it is a straightforward assumption that the town was laid out in grid form around the temple and also around the royal palace whose likely site was north of the temple, not far from the well-known stone tank.

On either side of the great causeway lie two shrines which are open to the four quarters and which have erroneously been called 'libraries', followed by two ponds which may be of later date than the town, one of which is faced in sandstone.

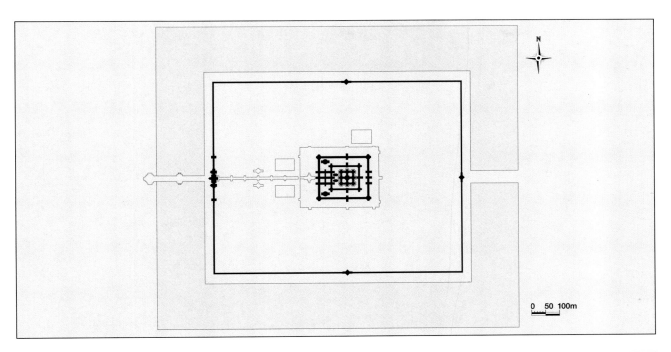

Opposite
The very large statue of Vishnu of more than four metres fits uncomfortably in its present position in the west entrance pavilion, suggesting it was formerly in the central shrine of the temple.

Left: Plans of Angkor Wat. That above showing the large moat surrounding the city; that below showing the central core in more detail.

Overleaf
Looking back down the causeway to the west entrance with the two so-called 'libraries' on either side.

Le massif central d'Angkor Vat,
vu du nord-ouest. Au premier plan,
la «bibliothèque» nord.

THE GREAT TEMPLE

Any description of Angkor Wat runs the risk of failing to do it justice. It can be seen from afar, but it only appears to the eye in its entirety and in wonderful perspective, at the moment when the viewer has crossed the western entrance pavilion of the town. In the early morning it can be shrouded in mist, at midday flooded in blinding light, whilst in the evening it presents an entrancing spectacle which gradually fades into a silhouette against the night sky.

To enter the temple through its main gate the visitor must first cross the 'town' and reach the end of the paved causeway, climb the stairway which leads to the elegant cruciform terrace (which was probably not part of the original design) and then proceed into the entrance pavilion, from which doorways on either side lead into the galleries of bas-relief friezes carved into the exterior wall of the third enclosure. Their total length is 500 metres of sculpture, two metres high, and covering all four walls of the temple, without including those in the two pavilions at the south-west and north-east corners. The overall plan is extremely well conceived. To the west on the south side, on a single 200-square metre panel, the terrible final battle of the great Indian epic *Mahabharata* is depicted. At the end of the gallery is the south-west corner pavilion whose interior is entirely sculpted in bas relief, with various episodes from Indian legend.

On reaching the temple and turning left towards the north, the visitor can admire the grand Battle of Lanka recounted in the *Ramayana*, the other great Indian epic which is still familiar today to everyone throughout South-East Asia. It is visually summarised in the scenes which decorate the north-east corner pavilion, some of which have not been elucidated, and may well be episodes which the Khmers added to the original.

On the south side of the temple, in the west section, the famous 'Historical Gallery' allows the visitor to marvel at King Suryavarman II on his throne surrounded by his counsellors, ministers and Brahmins. Further on, the great military parade wends its way, and is a device to show a series of portraits of the mightiest generals, the lords of the empire, and a further portrait of the king on his elephant, with minuscule inscriptions to record their names. Here too, on the east side of the same gallery, is the 'Gallery of Heaven and Hell', relating the judgement of Yama, god of the 'underworld'. It shows the celestial bliss of the lords in the company of *apsaras*, whilst the wicked undergo abominable torments, pictured in detail. Again, inscriptions are there to list the offences which deserved these punishments.

Naga balustrade and 'library' from the causeway, looking west.

Detail from the Churning of the Sea of Milk showing a high-ranking 36-headed asura *holding the head of the five-headed* naga *Vasuki.*

Opposite: Inner courtyard of the cruciform gallery, first storey.

Overleaf
Page 164: Detail of the pediment from the west entrance pavilion showing a battle scene from the Ramayana *between monkeys and* asuras.

Page 165: Details from the Ramayana *bas-reliefs of the north wing of the west gallery showing the Battle of Lanka.*
Left: Rama's brother Lakshmana is on the right, with the demon Vibhishana, with whom they had forged an alliance, behind him.
Right: Rama standing on the shoulders of Hanuman.

On entering the temple from the east and turning left, the viewer is plunged once more into Indian legend with the renowned 'Churning of the Sea of Milk' from which spurts the nectar of immortality. It is produced by Mount Mandara turned upside down and acting as a churn dasher, which oscillates with the serpent Vasuki wrapped round it acting as a rope, pulled alternately by the gods on one side and the demons on the other, for once acting in alliance with each other. Vishnu is twice present; first in his turtle *avatar* where he is the pivot of the mountain, and then in his normal shape on its summit. The composition, however, is not in exact conformity to the Indian narrative. Particularly noticeable is the unusual participation of Hanuman, the general of Rama's monkey allies. It is hard to say which is most admirable: the perfect symmetry of this 'picture', or the unbridled fantasy of the Khmer artists expressed in the proliferation of fish and aquatic animals which fill the sea and are caught up in the whirlpool of the churn (see pages 176-81 and endpapers).

To the north of the eastern entrance pavilion there are relief scenes of 'the Victory of Vishnu over the *Asura*' which are of much inferior quality to the others. This is because this section, like the eastern half of the north gallery, which shows the 'Victory of Krishna over the *Asura* Bana', was not carved during the period of Suryavarman II, probably due to lack of time, and was added only in the 16th century, to be precise, between Wednesday 8 September 1546 and Sunday 27 February 1564, in the course of a project to restore the temple which had been undertaken by two kings, or possibly only one. It is generally accepted, despite any real evidence of a link between him and the temple, that this was King Ang Chan, whose identity is revealed in the Royal Chronicles. It is probable, too, that the corner pavilions to the north-east and south-east would also have been adorned with relief carvings if the king had been able to finish his temple.

Lastly, the eastern part of the north gallery features a mammoth battle scene. In the midst of a tangled mass of warriors, the twenty-one major gods of the Brahmanical pantheon can be discerned, each in single combat with a demon.

Along the way, the visitor will have gone through the entrance pavilions of the four cardinal points, and noticed their triple passageways to the east and the west, and the single ones which point north and south. Each passage has a stairway outwards, with the salient exception of the axial stairway to the east, where it is lacking. This obvious anomaly poses a real problem, as it is most unlikely that no access had been provided at that particular spot. In fact, the continuous mouldings which cover it are so crude that they could only have been added at a much later period.

Right: A monkey struggles with an asura *in the Battle of Lanka from the* Ramayana, *west gallery of bas-reliefs.*

Far right: Ravana shakes Mount Kailasa, the abode of Shiva, south-west corner pavilion.

Far left: The death of Valin, having been shot by Rama's arrow.

Left: Detail from a battle scene from the Mahabharata.

The army of the Kauravas, with some of their commanders, march into the Battle of Kurukshetra. After an 18-day conflict all the Kauravas were killed. West gallery of bas-reliefs.

Overleaf
Left: Hand-to-hand fighting in the battle between the Kauravas (left) and the Pandavas (right).

Right: Pandava warriors with shields and spears.

171

Pages de gauche et de droite :
Détails du grand bas-relief du Ciel et des Enfers, galerie sud, côté est. Divers tourments infligés aux pécheurs par les sbires de Yama.

Pages suivantes :
Partie centrale du grand bas-relief du barattage de la Mer de Lait, galerie est, côté sud. Vishnu, au centre, devant le mont Mandara inversé qui sert de baraton, contrôle les mouvements des 92 asura (à sa gauche) et des 88 deva (à sa droite). Au-dessus apparaissent les apsara, nées du barattage. Au-dessous, les créatures vivant dans l'océan, plus ou moins extraordinaires, sont écrasées et décimées par le mouvement de la montagne.

Left: Hanuman, king of the monkey troops, commanding the team of devas *during the Churning of the Sea of Milk.*

Far left: Flying apsaras *created by the Churning of the Sea of Milk, east gallery.*

Overleaf
Denizens of the sea caught up in the churning.

Suryavarman II and Angkor Wat   179

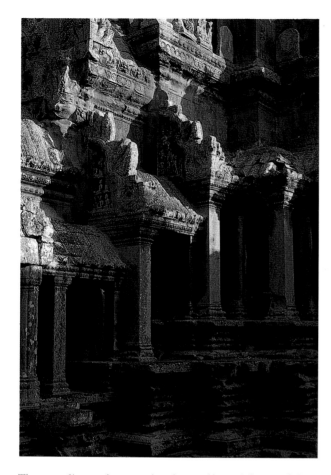

The ascending roofs connecting the cruciform cloister and the second level of the temple.

The three western passageways continue towards the east up stairways which lead to the famous 'cruciform cloister' with its four ponds, and its south side known as the 'Hall of the Thousand Buddhas' – so called because of the Khmers' pious deposits there, of a great number of statues over the last centuries. Today the hall is almost empty. The Curator of the Angkor monuments had had the best statues removed for protection at the beginning of the civil war, and the Khmer Rouge subsequently took away and destroyed almost everything that remained.

The north and south axial porches of this cloister gave access to 'libraries', smaller than those of the town, but like them in having four doorways, which is enough proof that they were not intended to house manuscripts. They are on quite a high raised pedestal, which allows them to be seen from the outside, above the galleries which contain the relief carvings. Before leaving the cloister which sits at this intermediate level, the visitor can observe the artistry and skill of the three roofed stairways which lead up to the second storey. The latter is surrounded by a peripheral gallery with blind walls to the exterior and must have housed numerous deities, as did the corner pavilions, built like real tower-shrines with four projecting porches.

Two small 'libraries' with four doorways stand in the western courtyard of this storey. A kind of footbridge on small cylindrical columns runs across the centre of the yard connecting the libraries with the entrance pavilion and the stairway of the central mass. The footbridge is undoubtedly later as its sides conceal previously carved surfaces. On the other three sides the courtyards are narrower and without buildings.

A further effort is needed to clamber up the 11-metre gradient of the central mass, up one of the four steep stairways, lined with beautiful string-walls, which lead to the top in a single flight. The upper storey has finally been reached, with its quincunx of five towers linked with galleries from which there is a view of the surrounding plain through the stone window bars which are admirably sculpted and lathe-turned. On the nearby walls and on the towers which soar into the sky, are yet more of the *apsaras*. The four doors of the main tower were once open, but were all walled up in the 14th or 15th centuries, and sculpted with Buddha images, thus transforming the shrine into a sort of *stupa*. The tower originally housed a statue of Vishnu, and its size would indicate that the statue was of monumental proportions. It has never been traced, but it is possible that the large statue nowadays worshipped in the intermediate pavilion of the town entrance is its ultimate *avatar*.

The magnificence of the architecture is everywhere enhanced by the extensive bas-reliefs finely chiselled on so many walls and door jambs, and on the foot of so many columns, on a multitude of pediments illustrating the glory of the various gods and their exploits. One may also try and imagine the temple as it was with all the divinities in their shrines which now seem like passageways because their doors have vanished, and the hundreds of priests attending to their needs.

THE AMBITION OF A GREAT CONQUEROR

The reign of Suryavarman II is marked by the resumption of close diplomatic relations with China, which had long been dormant. We learn from the Chinese Annals that the Khmer king sent 'embassies' there in 1116 and 1120. They seem to have had much more of an economic than a political or strategic focus.

From time immemorial the Khmers had quarrelled with their Cham neighbours. The independence of Vietnam, which had succeeded at the beginning of the tenth century in throwing off the yoke of Chinese domination, began to change the regional balance. From the reign of Suryavarman II, relations between the Khmer empire and Champa were to be completely altered, and there were to be no more of the localised surprise attacks which seem to have been the norm in former times. The Khmer king boldly stated his orders on Cham territory, which implies he had friends in one or several Cham kingdoms.

Suryavarman's designs seem here to have been particularly ambitious. It is not certain that he intended to 'annex' the land of Champa at the beginning of his reign, but it was from there that he was to wage war on Vietnam, dragging the Cham kings willy-nilly along in this hazardous venture. Furthermore, in 1145 towards the end of his reign, he placed Prince Harideva, the younger brother of one of his chief queens (herself a Cham) on the throne of the Cham king of Vijaya (in the region of present-day Qui-nhon) having previously killed the king. This deed provoked the fury of Jaya-Harivarman I, another Cham king, who killed Harideva in 1149 and proclaimed himself 'supreme king of the Cham kings', a title doubtless adopted to defy the Khmer king. It is from this time on that the unrelenting wars between Chams and Khmers began.

Suryavarman II did not content himself with waging war on the Vietnam front. He had no difficulty in preserving for the Khmer empire the provinces beyond the Dangrek mountains, as far as the region of Lopburi. He led his armies much further north in what is now Thailand, and well down into the Malay peninsula. The Chinese Annals give this approximate description of his empire in the mid-twelfth century: "Cambodia borders the southern frontiers of Champa to the north, the sea to the east, the kingdom of Pagan to the west and Grahi to the south". (The land of Grahi corresponds to the present-day regions of Chaiya and Nakhon Si Thammarat in Thailand).

The last years of Suryavarman II are shrouded in obscurity, and the date of his death is unknown. The final inscription which names him during his lifetime is dated 1145, but it is tempting to attribute one final campaign to him, which most probably ended in disaster, against Vietnam in 1150.

The 'Hall of the Thousand Buddhas' as it was in 1896 before their subsequent removal. (Photo: © British Library)

Some of the almost 2,000 apsaras *carved on the walls and columns throughout the temple.*

Left: Apsaras *in the north-west corner of courtyard of the second level.*

Overleaf
Left: View from the summit to the courtyard of the second level and beyond.

Right: The remaining Buddha images in the 'Hall of the Thousand Buddhas'.

An apsaras *from Thommanon.*

Opposite: The east entrance to Phnom Rung.

OTHER TEMPLES IN THE ANGKOR WAT STYLE

There is no mention in the inscriptions of the 'minor' temples of Thommanon and Chau Say Tevoda on either side of the causeway which ran between the royal palace of Angkor Thom and that of Jayavarman V. From a detailed stylistic study it appears that the former dates from the early years of Suryavarman's reign, and the latter was built towards its close. It should not however be forgotten that at the time these temples were built, this 'royal way' was not a significant feature, since the centre of the empire was undoubtedly on the site of Angkor Wat. Nothing indicates that they had been symmetrically planned from the outset, as they are not closely similar and Chau Say Tevoda seems somewhat the later of the two.

Far from there, and near the east bank of the East Baray, the very fine monument of Banteay Samre must have been erected in the same period by a high dignitary. However, we have no more documentary evidence on this temple than on the others. It is sited some 450 metres east of the *baray*, towards its south-east corner, and is like Angkor Wat in having an entrance causeway crossed by flights of stairs. The causeway is 200 metres long, and, again like Angkor Wat, the temple is preceded by a cruciform terrace. This author tends to believe that the terrace should be dated to the thirteenth century, but the causeway indicates that the temple was at the centre of a town, extending perhaps over some 80 hectares.

On the road from Angkor in present-day Thailand, some 60 kilometres before it reaches Phimai, there is the foot of an elongated hill which is called (for this reason) Phnom Rung. At least from the reign of Rajendravarman this hill had been a refuge for ascetics who had built several shrines on it. But in the twelfth century Narendraditya, a first cousin of Suryavarman, retired there after a glorious military career, and it is to him that is owed the major part of the Phnom Rung temple, whose restoration was completed by the Thai Fine Arts Department in 1988. Its siting at the top of Phnom Rung, the long causeway which leads to it, and the quality of the building, make it an important site in the former Khmer lands. Apart from this, the large *baray* extending at the foot of the hill and the temple of Muang Tam dating from the previous century, are an eloquent tribute to the former wealth of this region.

It is probably in Suryavarman's reign too, that the building of the great temple of Beng Mealea was at least begun. It lies at the foot of the southern cliff of Phnom Kulen, some 40 kilometres east of Angkor, on the road towards the 'great Preah Khan' which is some 60 kilometres further on, and is both a town and a temple complex whose history is virtually unknown. Beng Mealea is also on the way to Koh Ker, and was also the starting point of a canal which led to the Great Lake, and which, significantly, was also probably used to float the stone blocks from the nearby quarries, downstream to Angkor.

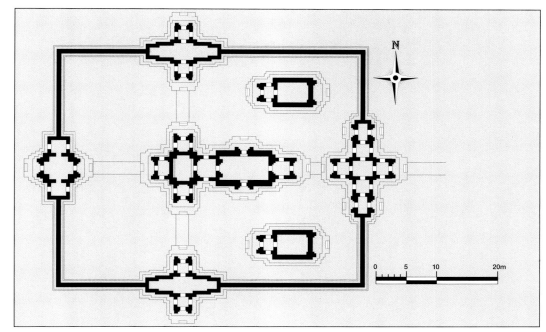

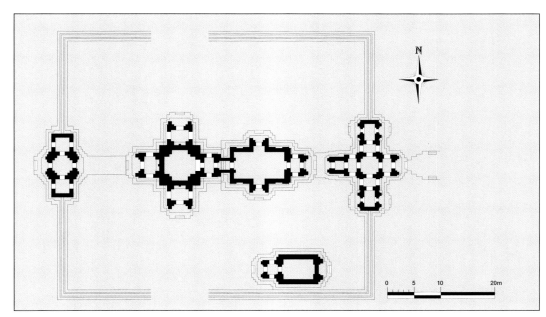

Two plans of 'minor' Angkor Wat period temples. Above: Chao Say Tevoda; below: Thommanon.

Left: The east entrance pavilion of Chao Say Tevoda.

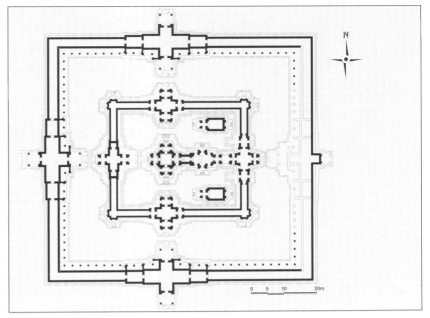

Aerial view of Banteay Samre. (Photo: Guy Nafilyan)

Above: Plan of Banteay Samre.

Left: The south pediment of the inner entrance pavilion, Banteay Samre, showing Rama riding on Hanuman, surrounded by monkey troops, from the Ramayana.

Opposite: North-eastern part of the inner enclosure showing the 'library', Banteay Samre.

Dancing apsaras *with musicians above the north entrance pavilion of the inner enclosure, Banteay Samre.*

Below: East pediment, north 'library', Banteay Samre. Vishnu reclines on a dragon, while above Brahma sits on a lotus coming from Vishnu's navel.

In its dimensions and in the care with which it was built, Beng Mealea is comparable with the greatest achievements of Angkor. Its ground plan is very similar to that of Angkor Wat, but it has an eastward orientation, and the group is a little more compact, and laid out at ground level. It is decidedly the work of a very powerful lord, but his name is unknown and not a single inscription has either been found on the site, or has even alluded to it. Only the style permits an approximate dating to the middle of the twelfth century. The decoration of the temple is particularly refined. The themes on its low relief carvings are mostly Vishnuite in their inspiration, but there are also Shivaite and Buddhist scenes. This is probably not due to 'syncretism' between Buddhism and Hinduism, but rather a sign of a succession of 'tenants'.

The town whose centre it occupied is surrounded by a moat without walls, measuring about 900 by 770 metres. Four major paved avenues lead to the gates of the temple, which has a large *baray* preceding it to the east, with the customary small shrine on the island raised in its centre. In the immediate proximity there are various slightly earlier and later shrines. There are some elements, such as the southern 'annexes' and the terraces on cylindrical columns, which indicate later modifications.

MAJOR ARCHITECTURAL PROJECTS AND RESTORATIONS: YASHOVARMAN II

On the death of Suryavarman II, around 1150 AD, the supreme crown passed to Yashovarman II, a king whose origin and accession to the throne are completely mysterious. For a long time it was assumed that between Suryavarman II and Yashovarman II, there could have intervened the reign of the father of the future Jayavarman VII: Dharanindravarman II. There is, in reality, no trace of such a reign. It is more likely that this particular person, with his royal title, never acceded to the supreme Khmer throne, but nevertheless it is possible that he ruled part of the empire, which was doubtless once again fragmented. As concerns Yashovarman II, it is a fact that his name does not appear in the 'genealogy' of Jayavarman VII, which shows that he was not of the family of Mahidharapura. Perhaps he sprang from a former lineage. The disturbances which we can guess at, towards the end of the reign of Suryavarman II, lead us to think that the accession of this king was not without its irregularities. Happenstance and also the will of his successor, who eliminated him brutally, have brought about a situation in which not a single inscription dating from Yashovarman's time, or even mentioning him, has come down to us.

While we know nothing of Yashovarman II other than the approximate date (1150 AD) of his accession, and the probable date of his death (1165), it is nevertheless a fact that great works of architecture were begun or continued during his almost 16-year reign. It is indeed unlikely that the temple of Beng Mealea, or lesser shrines such

Base of a pilaster from the south face of the west porch of the main sanctuary, Banteay Samre.

The feet of an apsaras *from Thommanon, characteristically turned to the side to avoid the sculptor having to tackle any awkward problems of perspective.*

as Thommanon and Chau Say Tevoda, or again Banteay Samre, were all completed by the death of Suryavarman II.

In a different context, it is tempting to attribute to Yashovarman II the restorations of the old temples of the Roluos group. It has long been observed that the central shrine of Bakong temple, despite a few archaic features, belongs to the 'style of Angkor Wat', as does at least one statue discovered on the site of Lolei. The attention given to these temples, so long after they had been built, is credible evidence that a descendant from the old lineages had reappeared on the royal throne. As this was definitely not Suryavarman II (otherwise the evidence would have survived), it could have been Yashovarman II, desiring in this way to attract to himself the favours of his great ancestors, whose deeds were still celebrated at the time.

There are some clues which give rise to the theory that Yashovarman II left the zone of Angkor Wat and set up his royal palace on the present site of Preah Khan temple. It is doubtless there that on his return from an expedition to Lavodaya (the present-day Lopburi in Thailand) he fell to one of his 'mandarins' who had rebelled, and who soon had himself crowned under the name of Tribhuvanadityavarman, at a date around 1165 AD. As soon as the future Jayavarman VII had learned of this violent event (as an inscription relates), he rushed from the Cham kingdom of Vijaya to support the legitimate king. It might be suspected too, that from this time on, but so far unsuccessfully, he coveted the supreme throne for himself. Tribhuvanaditya-varman was the only supreme king whom an inscription – unique in itself – accuses as an usurper. He was to reign at Angkor for some 12 years, and was to be eliminated in his turn by a king from Champa: Jaya-Indravarman IV. We have little idea of which monuments were built during his reign, and apart from the said inscription in Angkor itself, which was sculpted during the succeeding reign, the only surviving mention of his name is on a copper plate, found far away, south of Phnom Bayang, in today's southern Vietnam.

Meanwhile in 1177 AD the Cham king, Jaya-Indravarman IV, decided to launch a raid on Angkor, perhaps after being provoked by serious Khmer incursions on his territory. In fact this was not an easy enterprise. The Chinese Annals claim that the Chams forayed to Angkor over water, sailing up one of the branches of the Mekong to the Tonlé Sap river and on to the Great Lake, guided throughout by a Chinese pilot. But it is known that another armed force 'transported on chariots' boldly undertook the long march through the mountains between the two countries. It can be assumed that they were also joined by the Khmer kings who were Jaya-Indravarman's allies, and therefore enemies both of Tribhuvanadityavarman and of the future Jayavarman VII, and, although they are depicted on the bas-relief friezes, are all too often forgotten. Under the assault of these combined forces, Angkor was to fall, and its usurper king to lose his life. A new chapter of Khmer history was to open

The redented angle of the central sanctuary of Thommanon.

Two superposed pediments on the west entrance pavilion of Thommanon. The upper one shows Shiva as an ascetic.

Overleaf
The tower, sanctuary and 'library' of Thommanon was completely reconstructed in the 1960s.

Chapter seven
Angkor Thom

When the usurper Tribhuvanadityavarman seized power from Yashovarman II, around 1165 AD, a Khmer prince – the future Jayavarman VII – had rushed from the Cham kingdom of Vijaya to defend his king. By the time he arrived it was all over, and he had to suspend the struggle for some considerable while. He was resolutely encouraged towards the supreme throne by his chief spouse, Princess Jayarajadevi, and patiently awaited his time for more than twelve years, in whereabouts which remain obscure. When the news came from his country of the ruin of the usurper and the victory of the Cham enemy Jaya-Indravarman IV, Jayavarman immediately set out for Angkor with his army.

In Bayon temple, on a part of the bas-relief frieze of the southern gallery, the artists depict a huge naval battle between Khmers and Chams. It is commonly accepted that this was the battle which took place on the Great Lake and was the prelude to the reconquest of the capital, which is why it is given such prominence. But further bloody battles were to follow, until the last encounter and final victory, which probably had as its theatre the royal palace. Whether or not this was so, the battlefield became the site for the future temple of Preah Khan, and an inscription of Jayavarman VII which refers to it, speaks of a lake of blood. King Jaya-Indravarman himself perished there.

The victory gained the town of Yashodharapura for Jayavarman VII, but not the Khmer empire. The ensuing campaign which allowed him to gain control of it has all too often been termed a 'liberation'. This is unrealistic and markedly anachronistic: the inscriptions themselves assert that Jayavarman's task was to reunify an empire "shaded under many parasols", where each 'parasol' was, of course, a king. The pacification of the empire implies that each of the kings had to accept a new supreme ruler, and it may not have been plain sailing. In fact it was only in 1181, four years

Head of Jayavarman VII.

Opposite: Face towers on the upper terrace, Bayon.

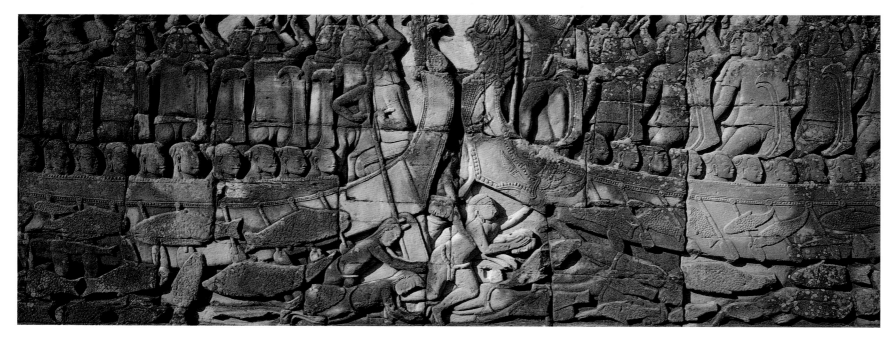

Cham warships in battle with the Khmers on the Great Lake, southern outer gallery, Bayon.

after the Cham incursion, that the supreme consecration of Jayavarman VII was celebrated, and there is proof positive that rebellions broke out some years later, not far from Angkor.

The names of his direct ancestors are known: his father was Dharanindravarman II, whom historians long considered one of the supreme kings of the period. This is, in fact, a rather remote possibility, but as the empire had split up into small kingdoms after the reign of Suryavarman II, or at the very least after that of Yashovarman II, it is quite possible that he was the ruler of one of the small 'independent' kingdoms at that time. Dharanindravarman was the son of Suryavarman II's mother's younger brother, and was thus a full first cousin of Suryavarman. This did not however confer any particular right to the supreme throne on him, and even less on his son. Jayavarman's mother, Jayarajacudamani, was the daughter of a king named Harshavarman, who was probably one of the minor Khmer kings, and is not otherwise mentioned.

Jayavarman VII often gives the impression of being better-known than other Khmer kings, perhaps on account of the 'portrait-statues', as Cœdès dubs them, which show him meditating. In another context, his abundant pious works, in particular the hospitals, which are described in two great Sanskrit poems, are a tribute to the humanity of this king who seems overwhelmingly devoted to the well-being of his subjects. It should not be forgotten, however, that Jayavarman spent the first half of his life engaged in warfare in the Cham kingdom of Vijaya, and that he had to lead many campaigns to restore the unity of his seriously fragmented empire, before having himself crowned as supreme king in 1181.

After the coronation, Jayavarman's empire had by no means acquired the degree of stability it would have needed to avoid further struggle to keep it together. Through a Cham inscription, we learn – almost accidentally – that the city of Malyang, believed to be in the region of today's Battambang, had rebelled several times. In the end, he sent a young Cham prince, Vidyanandana, to put down the rebellion. Vidyanandana had followed Jayavarman to the court of Angkor "from his earliest youth", and had been personally trained by the king in the martial arts. For Jayavarman to have entrusted such a campaign to a Cham prince implies a certain lack of confidence in his Khmer generals. After its successful conclusion, he was to bestow the important title of *yuvaraja* ('crown prince') on Vidyanandana.

TA PROHM

Apart from the wars, the account of Jayavarman's reign could be amply documented simply by listing the monuments he commissioned. It should always be remembered, however, that some of them were probably only initiated during his reign, and that all were developed, sometimes in several phases, over more than a century. In sum, it is often difficult to divide those he really built from those which are due to his successors.

In the former category, first mention should be made of the great temple-monastery of Ta Prohm, whose original name was Rajavihara – 'the monastery of the King'. It was surrounded by a town which is now only forest and scrub. Its enclosure delineated an area of sixty hectares and was built in the following century, while the temple itself occupies an area of barely one hectare. The inscription informs us that the monastery employed 12,640 people in total, and that to feed this multitude no less than 79,365 people worked in the villages attached to the temple.

The main divinity of Ta Prohm was the 'Mother of the Buddhas', Prajñaparamita: the 'Perfection of Wisdom', and was sculpted in the image of Jayavarman VII's mother. Two subsidiary temples housed the statues of gods similarly carved as portraits of the king's two *gurus*, his elder brother Jayakirti and the Brahmin Jayamangalartha. Apart from these, there were 260 gods ensconced in the various shrines of this complex temple in a pattern which is difficult to retrace today. Their 'eyes were opened' in 1186 AD. An additional function of the temple was to administer the royal supplies for the 102 hospitals scattered throughout the empire and which will be described below.

The 'Angkor Conservancy' took the decision to leave Ta Prohm in a carefully preserved 'natural state' to allow visitors to experience the excitement of the first discoverers of Angkor.

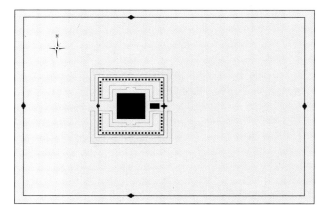

Overall plan of the city of Ta Prohm.

Above: Aerial view of Ta Prohm.

Plans of Ta Prohm.
Right: As the temple was probably originally conceived.

Below: As the temple exists today.

Opposite: Bas-reliefs on either side of the east entrance enclosure showing scenes from the life of the Buddha.

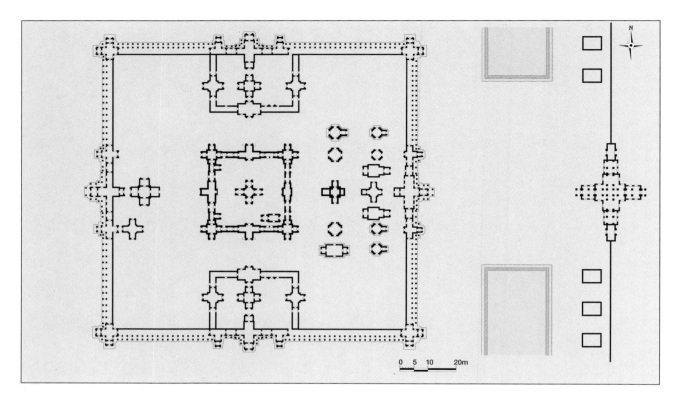

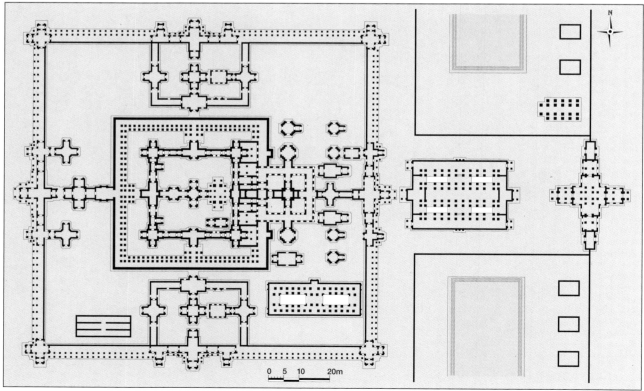

Detail from the lintel showing the Great Departure of Siddartha Gautama, the future Buddha, when he left his father's palace at night with angels carrying his horse in order to avoid any noise.

Left: Overgrown sanctuary tower and silk cotton tree.

Opposite: Doorway framed by the aerial roots of strangler figs.

Overleaf
Central group of towers, Ta Prohm.

Strangler fig enclosing naga *heads.*

Opposite: Collapsed gallery in the second enclosure.

Overleaf
Left: Doorframe within the inner enclosure.

Right: Roundels on pilasters on the south side of the west entrance are unusual in design. In particular, that at left shows an animal which bears a striking resemblance to a stegasaurus.

South-west corner tower of the inner enclosure, Ta Prohm.

Opposite: Interior of the west entrance of the second enclosure.

One of the asuras *holding the body of a giant* naga *at the west entrance to Preah Khan.*

THE UNIVERSITY OF PREAH KHAN AND ITS SUBSIDIARY TEMPLES

Another major temple was then built on land which was probably the site of the palace of Jayavarman's immediate predecessors, and was the scene of the battle which marked the fall of Angkor to the Cham onslaughts. Its enclosure surrounded a town of 56 hectares, somewhat smaller than that of Ta Prohm although the temple itself is about the same length but considerably wider, covering a rectangle of 200 metres by 175. It was perhaps a kind of university rather than a mere monastery, with numerous teachers and students. Unfortunately the lines of the inscription which refer to it have almost all been lost, but they indicate that more than a thousand teachers were installed there. As at Ta Prohm, a multitude of people worked in the temple for a much larger number of deities, and needed a great deal of land for their sustenance. 97,840 labourers produced approximately ten tonnes of white rice per day, among other produce, and if the daily ration is estimated at 650 grams, it can be seen that some fifteen thousand people could be fed.

Preah Khan temple is particularly complex and has more shrines even than Ta Prohm, but the epigraphy in this case reveals in some detail which divinity resided in each cella, thus allowing us to understand its structure. It was a veritable pantheon of Buddhist, Shivaite and Vishnuite gods, not to mention the guardian spirits of the land.

At the centre, of course, there was the Buddhist temple – the most important. Its principal statue was the Boddhisattva Lokeshvara, carved in the likeness of Jayavarman's father, and consecrated in 1191 AD. Around it were 282 secondary deities which, besides the gods of the Buddhist pantheon, included various recently deceased dignitaries who had become tutelary spirits of their family line, and Khmer heroes such as Arjuna and Sridhara from Devapura, who had died defending the palace of Yashovarman II when it was attacked by Tribhuvanadityavarman.

In front of the temple there was, however, the shrine of the god Tribhuvanavarmesvara, and it is tempting to relate this name with that of the 'usurper' king, Tribhuvanadityavarman, especially in view of the fact that the temple was built over his former palace. It should not be forgotten that, once crowned, a Khmer king became the protector of his country, whatever his past history.

To the south of the central complex was the temple of the former kings, with the spirit of King Yashovarman II at its centre, surrounded by 32 deities, heroes and major personalities. Later, however, following the death of Jayavarman VII, Yashovarman probably gave way to the great king, since his name is to be found in one of the minor shrines.

To the west, and opening westwards as at Angkor Wat, there was a Vishnu temple with 30 statues of his main *avatar* and of the divinities normally associated with him. At the centre of this temple the god Champesvara was enthroned. This name is indeed evocative of the rival nation which the Khmers, with mixed fortunes, had tried to annex, but is in fact a form of Vishnu known through older inscriptions both in India and in Cambodia.

To the north of the central complex there was a Shiva temple which housed a total of 40 deities. In the central spot, and exceptionally rare in Hindu iconography, the footprints of Shiva were venerated.

Within the temple precincts there were 42 further divinities of lesser rank, entrusted with the protection of the walkways and entrances and the rice granary, whilst the hospital and its gods were probably outside the enclosure of the city.

One of the 5-metre tall garudas *who surround the outer walls of Preah Khan.*

Left: The enigmatic, two-tiered, round-columned building whose exact purpose is unclear. Possibly it was a rice granary.

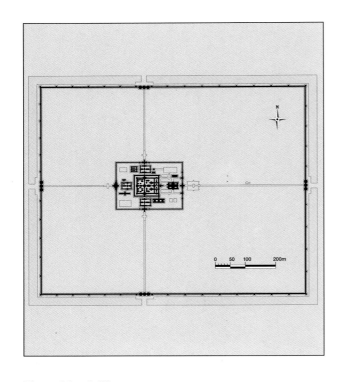

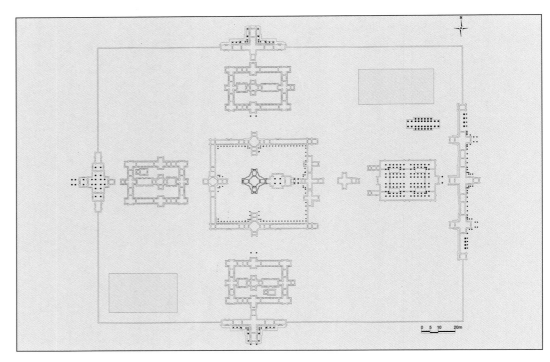

Plans of Preah Khan.
Above: The city.
Right: The temple as originally conceived.
Below: The temple as it is now.

Opposite above: Two lions guard the east entrance to Preah Khan.

Opposite below left: A freize of apsaras *from the 'Hall of Dancers'.*

Opposite below right: A row of rishis *in niches on the wall of a 'cell' in the inner enclosure.*

Overleaf
Galleries on the east-west axis.

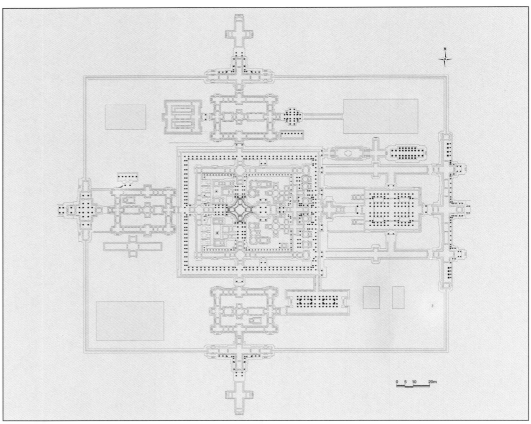

220

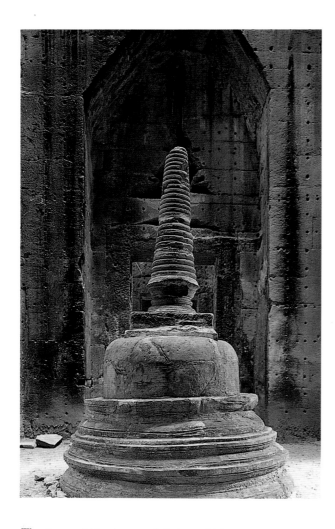

The stupa *within the central shrine, which in the 15th or 16th century replaced the statue of Lokeshvara, probably broken in the 13th century.*

Right: The central shrine with headless seated statue and stupa *behind. Note the holes in the walls which were used to affix gold-plated brass plaques.*

Above and left: Statue of princess praying to the Buddha, Bayon style, end 12th-early-13th century. (Musée Guimet)

To provide an indispensable final touch to this religious complex, Jayavarman ordered the construction of a substantial *baray* to the east of the town. It is the Jayatataka, three and a half kilometres long and 900 metres wide, and is nowadays in a dried-out state. In its centre, on a 300 metre square 'island', the striking group today known as Neak Pean was built. The name translates as 'entwined serpents', after the twin snakes wrapped around the base of the main sanctuary.

The main feature of the 'island' is thirteen areas of water, five of which are visible as carved cruciform ponds which have been restored. The central, 70 metre square pond is flanked at the four cardinal points by smaller square ponds which are at least theoretically able to receive the waters of the central pond through gargoyles sheltered by sandstone chapels, and carved with a human head to the east, a lion to the south, a horse to the west and an elephant to the north. In the middle of the central pond is the only sanctuary-tower of the group, rising from a circular base. It is in sandstone, and of relatively modest proportions. Eight further ponds, which lack a masonry facing, completed the rest of the island: four of them are complex in shape, and quite difficult to retrace. A wall surrounded the whole group, and many Buddhist artefacts have been found there. In the central pond itself, to the west, a statue of reclining Vishnu has been discovered, and to the north, some Shivaite *linga*. To the south there was an image damaged beyond recognition, while to the east there is the famous sculpture of the horse Balaha.

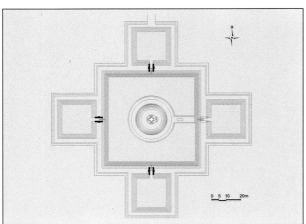

Plan of Neak Pean showing the five visible ponds.

Above: A deep relief of Lokeshvara on the southern blind door of the sanctuary of Neak Pean.

Right: Detail of pediment with a flying apsaras.

Opposite: The central sanctuary and pond of Neak Pean.

The fountain head of the east chapel, Neak Pean.

Right: The horse Balaha, a manifestation of Lokeshvara rescuing shipwrecked sailors.

Opposite: The inner enclosure of Ta Som.

It has been claimed that the Neak Pean group is a representation of the Buddhist Anavatapta, a miraculous lake in the Himalayas which heals all illnesses and from which spring four rivers through the mouths of a lion, an elephant, a horse and an ox. This almost matches our site, except that the ox is replaced by a man. But it does not correspond to the words of the Preah Khan stele: the original name was Rajyasri – 'the fortune of the kingdom' – and the site was clearly Hinduist. The supposition must therefore be that it was given its Buddhist character during the modifications which must have occurred in the first half of the thirteenth century. These included the walling-in of the south, west and north gates of the main shrine with stones carved with images of Lokeshvara, and probably the group of the horse Balaha. There remains the indubitable fact that the definitive aspect of this unique site in the Khmer country was intended to evoke a specific place. The key to the enigma, unless it is purely Khmer, might well be discovered more or less accidentally in Indian literature.

To the east of the Jayatataka was the temple of Ta Som, famous for the tower carved with faces of its western entrance pavilion, until recently wreathed in the branches and roots of a banyan tree. It was perhaps the temple mentioned as Gaurasrigajaratna – 'the jewel of the propitious white elephant', which housed a total of 22 divinities. The stele also records the presence in the Preah Khan group of a Yogindravihara ('monastery of the king of the *yogin*'), in which, it relates, were ensconced 16 deities, the same number as inhabited each of the two small ponds nearby. It has not yet been identified.

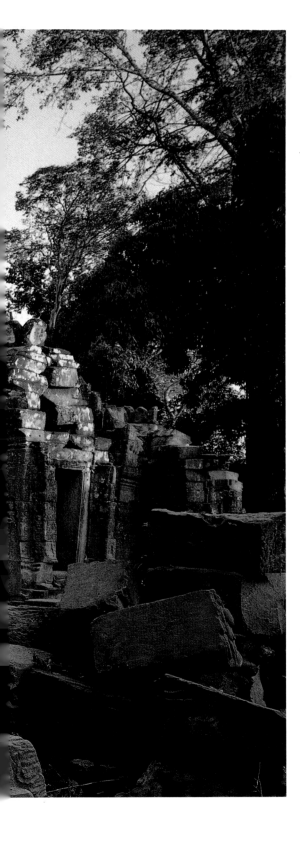

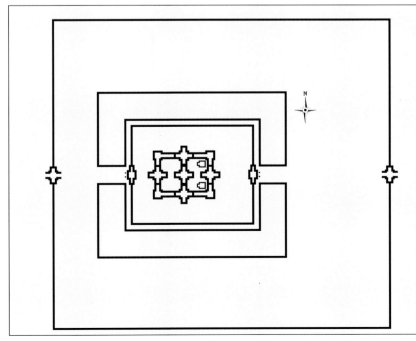

The south pediment of the west entrance pavilion with two rows of disciples of the Buddha, Ta Som.

Left: Plan of Ta Som.

Opposite: The inner enclosure of Ta Som from the second enclosure.

Overleaf
Srah Srang from the landing stage.

THE TEMPLE OF BANTEAY KDEI AND SRAH SRANG POOL

It has long been thought that Banteay Kdei was the shrine which the inscriptions called 'the Eastern Buddha'. In fact the 'Eastern Buddha' was doubtless much further to the east of Angkor, and should be sought in large complexes such as the Kompong Svay Preah Khan, or Beng Mealea.

As luck would have it, no precious inscribed stele has been found in this temple, as compared with those of Ta Prohm or Preah Khan, so Banteay Kdei consequently seems more mysterious. Its sheer size would, however, indicate a kingly attribution. It was built over the ruins of a former Buddhist temple, probably the work of Kavindrarimathana – Rajendravarman's architect – and elements of which are known to have been incorporated in the subsequent shrine. It was originally on quite a small scale, but was soon enlarged considerably, and given an exterior enclosure of comparable size to that of Ta Prohm. It had thus become the centre of a new walled town.

It was probably at the same time as these enlargements were begun, that a decision was made to renew the old Srah Srang *baray*, which lay east of Banteay Kdei and had been dug out by the same architect, Kavindrarimathana. On his accession, Jayavarman VII effected a magnificent remodelling of the former pond, shortening it somewhat, but facing its entire length and breadth with sandstone and laterite stairways. He also added a graceful terrace which can be seen in the axis of Banteay Kdei (not in that of the *baray*). It was from then on that the pond lived up to its modern name: Srah Srang, meaning 'the royal bath'.

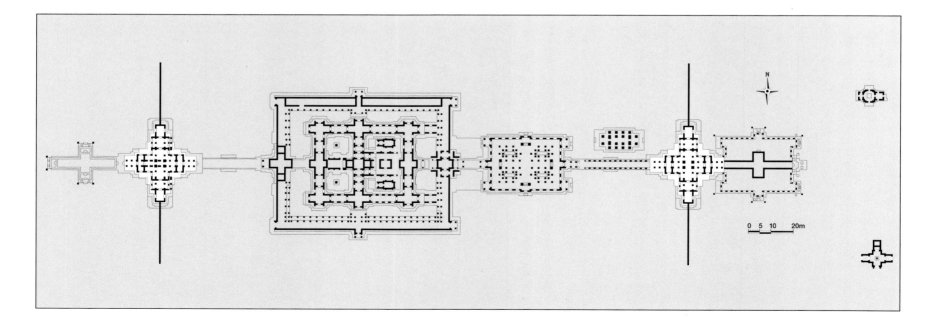

TA NEI

Ta Nei is a small temple not far from the western dike of the East Baray, halfway between Ta Prohm and Preah Khan. The only practicable access route was from the south, since the wall built by Jayaviravarman blocked it off to the north. Today it is off the beaten track, but it would originally have been circled with villages.

It dates from the early years of the reign and differs from the great temples of the period through having undergone few subsequent modifications. It is also distinguished by two long 'tank moats' running along its north and south sides. There is no evidence that it was a royal commission.

Devata *in niche, Ta Nei.*

Left: The west entrance pavilion, Ta Nei.

Opposite far left: Disciples of the Buddha are all that remain of a defaced pediment over the south door of the east entrance, Banteay Kdei.

Opposite left: The main west-east axis of Banteay Kdei.

Opposite: The 'Hall of Dancers' at Banteay Chhmar has a complex iconography. Unusual elements include the half-human, half-bird dancers, rishis and Brahma.

Overleaf
Face tower in the inner enclosure, Banteay Chhmar.

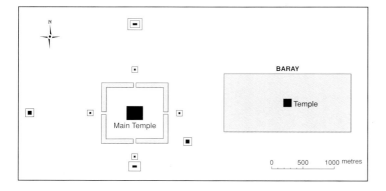

Plan of Banteay Chhmar showing the town with the main temple, surrounded by moats, other shrines and baray.

BANTEAY CHHMAR

Slightly more than a hundred kilometres north-west of Angkor as the crow flies, and not far from the frontier of present-day Thailand, the town and temple of Banteay Chhmar, together with their *baray* and several peripheral temples, make up an extensive site. It is odd that it should have been placed in this particularly inhospitable location which seems to have been called 'the sand country' in former times, and where no earlier monument has been reported. On the basis of a secondary inscription the theory has been advanced that the temple was dedicated to a son of Jayavarman VII, but in fact it may well have been built following the death of Rajapatindralakshmi, the paternal grandmother of the king, on her endowed land. This would indicate a starting date for the building of the temple between 1186 and 1191, which are, respectively, the dates of the consecration of the gods at Ta Prohm and Preah Khan.

The town is slightly smaller than the one which surrounded Preah Khan, but, unlike Ta Prohm, it was clearly conceived as a city, since it is surrounded by a 65-metre wide moat. To the east there is a rather inelegant 'house of fire'. The central sacred complex, however, is considerably larger and is enclosed by a wall which measures 250 by 190 metres. The wall is flanked by a gallery which houses a splendid series of bas-relief friezes. As at Bayon, they mainly depict battle scenes on land and water, but there are also illustrations of obscure legends. In addition, to the west, there is a remarkable sequence of eight large Lokeshvaras in quite a good state of preservation and illustrating the divinity with between four and 32 arms, and one to 16 heads.

The distribution of the shrines in the enclosure is similar to that at Preah Khan and Ta Prohm: there is a central group inside a series of enclosures in the shape of a long rectangle measuring 170 metres by 40. It was seemingly dedicated to Buddha. To the north, west and south are three separate temples which probably housed Shiva, Vishnu and the spirits of former kings, as at Preah Khan. The main shrine of the west temple is on a 3.7 metre high base and would have been similar to the one built during the initial phase of Bayon.

There are towers carved with faces, and others which remain blank, obviously following some chronological order, but many have collapsed and thus cannot be identified sequentially. The central shrine does not have a face tower carved and must be roughly contemporary with that of Preah Khan, whilst those of the temples to the south have carved faces and are probably no earlier than the twelfth century.

On the outskirts of the town there are eight shrines, each with a tower carved with faces, within single or double enclosures, but none has yielded an inscription. To the east of the temple there is a 1700 metre long *baray* with a westward landing stage running along the town's east entrance and quite noticeably off-centre towards the south. The *baray*, as usual, has a central island-temple, but paradoxically in this case it does not face in the direction which might have been expected.

PRASAT TOR

Among the many buildings of Jayavarman's reign is Prasat Tor, a small laterite temple at the north-east corner of the East Baray. It was indeed one of the few temples to Shiva built during the period, apart from those which were integrated with the great royal temples. At the beginning of his reign, Jayavarman VII installed an 'incomparable gold statue' (probably gilt bronze) cast in the image of his maternal grandfather, Harshavarman. The god which the statue represented is unfortunately not known, nor the reason for its presence there, but it can be speculated that there was a special connection linking Harshavarman, and consequently his grandson, with the hereditary owners of Prasat Tor.

Above: The partly collapsed south gallery of Banteay Chhmar, showing the battle of the Chams.

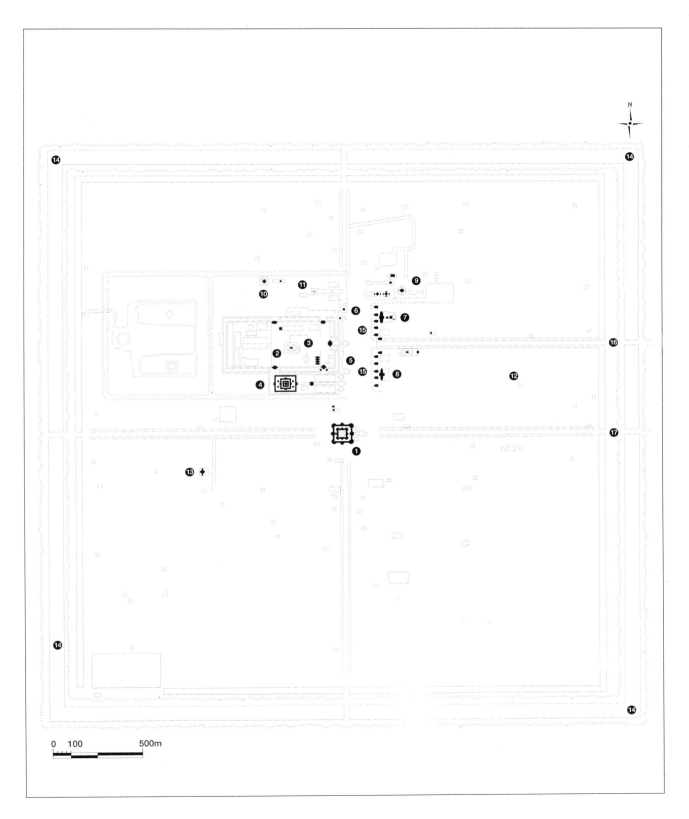

Angkor Thom

1   Bayon
2   Royal Palace
3   Phimeanakas
4   Bapuon
5   Elephant Terrace
6   Terrace of Leper King
7   North Khleang
8   South Khleang
9   Preah Pithu
10 Preah Palilay
11 Tep Pranam
12 Mangalartha
13 Monument 486
14 Prasat Chrung
15 Prasats Suor Prat
16 Victory Gate
17 Eastern Gate

The small rectangles shown on
the plan are the foundations of
Buddhist buildings, whose
upper parts in wood or
masonry have long since
disappeared.

*Opposite: The south-east Prasat
Chrung, one of four at each corner of
Angkor Thom. The pediment shows
Lokeshvara, to whom this temple is
dedicated.*

Guardian lion at the east entrance to the Bayon.

Opposite
Main picture: South gate of Angkor Thom.

Above centre: Deva *holding the body of the* naga *from the north gate of Angkor Thom.*

Above right: The last figure in the row of those holding the naga's *body, north gate.*

Below right: Asuras *from the south gate, Angkor Thom.*

THE GREAT CAPITAL: ANGKOR THOM

At some point Jayavarman VII decided to build his own capital, and it can be taken that this was right from the beginning of his reign, even if Preah Khan, with its resident gods, might have the appearance of a state temple. The town's enclosure is a huge square, three kilometres on one side, and delineates what is now called Angkor Thom - 'the great capital'. It has five monumental gateways, four of which correspond to the cardinal points of Bayon temple, and the fifth opens directly on to the royal palace via a triumphal way, recalling that of the former capital of Yashovarman I. Over and above their symbolic value, the town walls were defensive in nature, as confirmed explicitly in an inscription. They are eight metres high and have an interior earth bank along their entire length which acted both as a patrol path and an additional sloping fortification. To the exterior they were lined with a moat one hundred metres wide. The monumental gateways were apparently first built in the classical manner, and only in a subsequent phase adorned with the carved faces which characterise their present appearance.

The gates led outwards to the embanked causeways across the moat, which are bordered by the renowned snakes, grasped by divine beings. The author Paul Mus advanced the hypothesis that this was an illustration of the well-known 'Churning of the Sea of Milk' which is a frequent motif of Khmer art. While this is initially plausible, an alternative explanation - in view of the admirable images of the god Indra on his three-headed elephant which emphasise the royal character of the gateways - might be that of Jean Boisselier, namely that the snakes are the guardians of the capital's wealth.

At each corner of the walled city there is a sanctuary tower: the Prasat Chrung ('shrine of the angles'), each of which houses a stele engraved with a poem in honour of the king. Each has a different author, as did those of the four stelae of the East Baray at the time of Yashovarman I.

A FOREST OF HEADS: BAYON TEMPLE

At the centre of the town the state temple, Bayon, has given rise to much speculation, with its proliferation of towers carved with faces. It has been variously deemed to be a temple to Shiva, to Brahma or to Buddha. Nowadays it is known to be all of these and much more, like Preah Khan, and based on a similar plan, although somewhat 'compressed' in scale. It is in fact a pantheon, enshrining – or intended to enshrine – the whole gamut of deities worshipped in the empire of Jayavarman VII, which included not only the territory of the Khmers but also that of the vassal kingdoms in

Champa and elsewhere. As a pantheon, Bayon is more easily understood than Preah Khan, since it was the central mountain, the state temple.

The towers carved with faces seem only to have surmounted the shrines on the second and third storeys, and it is unlikely that they were present on the summits of the gate-lodges and those of the corner towers of the first enclosure. Attempts have sometimes been made to discern symbolic significance in the number of the towers or of their carved faces, but the truth is that these numbers increased during successive remodellings, and it therefore seems unproductive to look for any special numerical significance.

It must be admitted that Bayon, as it appears today, is a bewildering architectural tangle; a far cry from the pure classical order of Angkor Wat. It has long been thought that it was the product of several phases of construction. As far back as 1927, Henri Parmentier described it thus: "In its present state the monument evokes a strange impression of piling up and squeezing in. The towers are jumbled up against each other, the buildings are too close together to allow free passage, the courtyards are stifling, lightless wells." But the strange belief that a Khmer temple had to be completed during a particular reign was a major handicap to his interpretation, and it prevented any genuine attempt to discern what the original architect had really planned to build and symbolise. Nevertheless it is essential to discover the original intention, in view of the known fact that this sacred space was the State temple of several successive kings, whose religious convictions underwent a transition from an initial Mahayana Buddhism, to an aggressive form of Hinduism, and then reverted to the primordial Buddhism of the Ravada. In the next chapter it will be argued that these major changes, both in the general plan of the monument, and in the nature of the deities worshipped there, have historical as well as religious causes.

A walk through Bayon, noting on the way the relative age of its different parts, will afford a chance to trace its history. At ground level it is 156 metres long and 141 metres wide, smaller than Angkor Wat, and a little larger than Bapuon. A huge terrace, 72 metres long, stretches to the east of the monument. It is elevated at the centre, forming a walkway which broadens into a cruciform passage giving onto a flight of steps, and then into a terrace of foliated cusps whose north and south projections also end in flights of steps. There are traces of large ponds to the north and south of this terrace, but they are probably later additions.

The sacred compound is within a walled enclosure which forms an outward-facing gallery whose roof has collapsed. It has the usual four monumental entrance pavilions and corner pavilions, all built to the same configuration. The gallery wall is punctuated by a total of twenty doorways. There are two at the eastern extremities leading to the stairways of the 'libraries', although this was perhaps not the original intention as the latter are later additions. Two other doorways open symmetrically to

Aerial view of the Bayon.
(Photo: Claude Jacques)

Right: Plan showing the first stage of the Bayon.

the west, but their function is obscure, while on each of the four sides there are four further doorways, which in former times allowed access to what the Khmers have called *kuti*, or 'cells'. 'Chapels' would be quite a fair translation of the term, as the traditional rendering -'connecting rooms'- introduces a notion which is definitely misleading. Nowadays all that remains of them is a few traces at ground level. They are of irregular and uncertain shape and eight of them have flights of stairs allowing direct access from the outside, through the gallery of the relief friezes. As we shall see, these chapels were to be demolished in the thirteenth century, and their access doors walled up. Inscriptions on their door jambs in the gallery reveal that they originally housed the great Buddhist guardian divinities which Jayavarman VII had set up in the major towns of his empire, together with prominent local deities. Their former appearance can only be guessed at, but they were probably as stoutly built as the rest of the temple.

The gallery walls are adorned with relief friezes as at Angkor Wat, but reflect markedly different themes. There are military parades, battles on land and water, scenes from everyday life and religious ritual. In the context of the temple their interpretation gives rise to occasional problems, but they are a precious record of Khmer life and some compensation for the lost literature of the time.

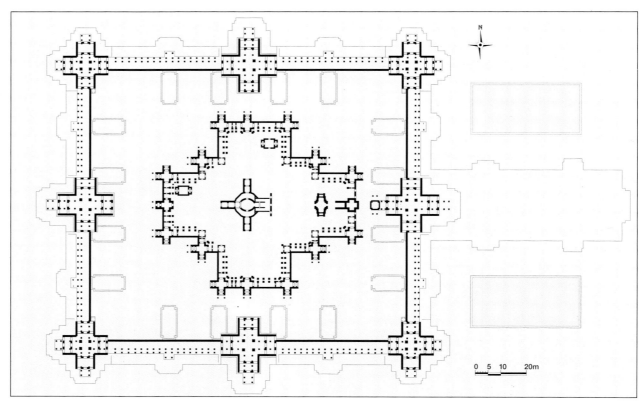

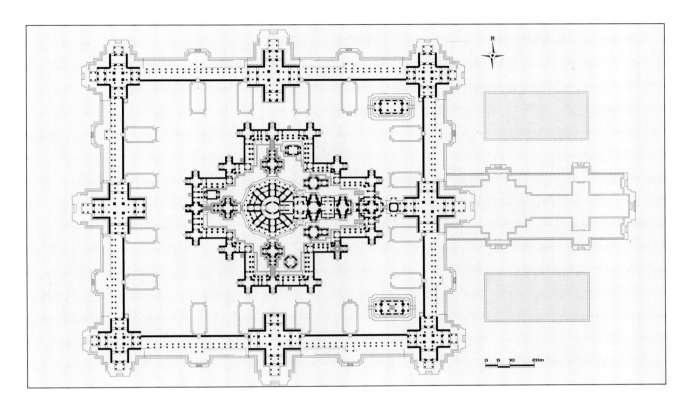

The second stage of the Bayon.

Below: The third stage.

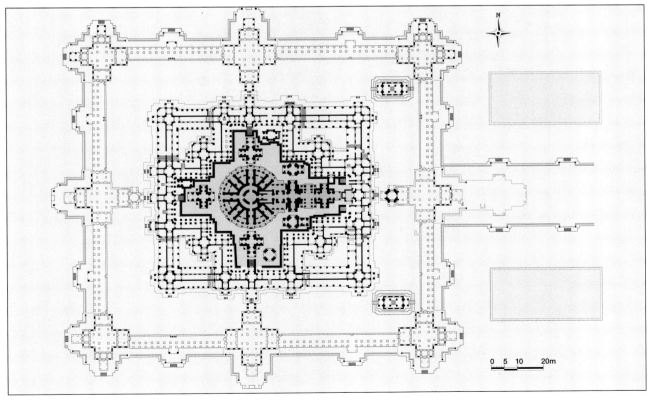

Devata *from the central sanctuary of Bayon.*

Opposite: The original inner galleries with the later upper terrace rising above.

In the north-east and south-west corners of this bottom storey, 'libraries' opening to the east and west can still be seen. They are perched on a tall plinth, and there is general agreement that they were built during the final phase of Bayon's construction, which this author dates to the second half of the thirteenth century, probably at the time the chapels were demolished.

Access to the second storey is via a short stairway. It is the most difficult of all to interpret, as it underwent the greatest number of subsequent additions, but the consensus is that the original plan was cruciform with foliated cusps, which implies that the corners of the gallery, which is now rectangular, were all later additions. Indeed their floors are some three metres below the second storey platform. The gallery-enclosure has, at each of its protruding or recessed angles, a sanctuary tower carved with faces, regardless of when each was built. It is evident, too, that the two shrines which are today squashed between the gallery and the wall of the third storey in its projection to the north and to the west, are part of the original design. Moreover, the fact that they were preserved despite subsequent modifications implies that they must have housed divinities which were venerated with particular fervour. Together with the gallery, they are all that remains of this storey, which probably originally included other places of worship.

After modification to its rectangular shape, the gallery was carved with reliefs, doubtless during the second half of the thirteenth century. The irregular shapes of the site made it imperative for the sculptors to carve a series of small scenes, the exact subjects of which have more often than not remained obscure. It is nevertheless of interest to observe that one of them already recounts the legend of the leper king.

To reach the top storey, there is a choice of five steep stairways: two to the east and one on each of the other sides. The eastern ones straddle the eastern tower of the second storey and in fact replace a single stairway which should have been in the centre but which subsequent remodellings have buried.

On reaching the top, the visitor is truly in another world. To walk around the central mass is to be under the gaze of dozens of faces looking down from every side with serene expressions and enigmatic smiles. The main sanctuary rises above the top terrace and appears to have an oval layout. The ground plan however reveals that the original design was cruciform, as elsewhere in the temple, and that the corners were rounded off at a later date by the addition of a series of radiating 'chapels'.

Each arm of the original cross projects into a tower, located where one would expect to find the gate-lodges: indeed the eastern one is a double tower. Two shrines stand on either side of this eastern forepart, built on the same ground-plan, as mirror-images of each other. They do not have towers and consequently are not carved with

faces. A tower with carved faces was built on the terrace to the south, and its function remains obscure. The top terrace itself, even with its subsequent widening, leaves little room for a crowd of any size to move around it.

The central sanctuary was naturally where the Buddha was enthroned. In the following century, when Jayavarman VIII ordered the systematic destruction of the Master's effigies, this statue was smashed and thrown into the well which marked the axis of the temple (and thus that of the world). The pieces have been retrieved and restored, and the statue, which is 3.6 metres high, can now be admired on a terrace near the royal square. It is plausible that one of the famous statues of Jayavarman VII in meditation was placed in the shrine which functioned as an ante-chapel to the main sanctuary. This is a far cry from the concept of a *Buddharaja* incarnating the king, dreamt up by authors as a parallel to their equally imaginary *Devaraja*.

The former kings, particularly the ancestors of Jayavarman's lineage, were venerated in the southern hall of the central structure and in the shrines which lead to it from the south. Among these was the 'God of Phimai', who should perhaps be recognised as one of Jayavarman's ancestors, and who was ensconced in the shrine in front of the central structure. To the west there was an effigy of Vishnu worshipped under the name of Harivarmesvara, which echoes the name of the Cham king Harivarman and Vijaya, and gives rise to the speculation that the god was installed at a time when Jayavarman believed he was still in control of Champa. In front of it stood a statue of Champesvara, a form of Vishnu, to whom a renowned temple, now lost, had long been venerated in the land of the Khmers. Finally, to the north, there would have been a Shiva shrine. Its inscription, and the statue it contained, have disappeared, but the tower in front of it housed the god Bhadresvara, the well-known form of Shiva worshipped at Wat Phu. It should be noted in passing that all this information comes from the inscriptions, the statues themselves having long since vanished.

The omnipresent carvings of Bayon have scarcely been mentioned. Here, as elsewhere, are *apsaras* sculpted on the columns in twos and threes, and *devata* on the walls and sanctuary pediments. As with all the temples of the period, the images of Buddha have disappeared: there remains only a figure of Lokeshvara, miraculously passed over in the wholesale destruction of the succeeding reign, on a pediment of one of the corner towers on the second level. Its discovery in 1925 prompted Louis Finot to affirm for the first time that the temple was Buddhist, which however is only partially true.

In its original state, Bayon was indeed very different from what can be seen today. The central mass, fronted by a tower, had been built on a cruciform plan, and looked down over the courtyard which lay between the galleries of the second level, as the terrace of the topmost storey did not exist. It must have looked rather like the western

Left: The start of a cockfight in which the two combatants are shown to each other, while so-called 'Chinese' bet over them.

Below: A game of chess.

Opposite: Detail of the previous panel with a camp follower starting a cooking fire, eastern outer gallery.

sanctuary at Banteay Chhmar, for example, or like those of some later temples in Cambodia and Thailand, where steep stairways up all four sides led to its shrines. The external enclosure wall had perhaps not yet been carved with relief friezes, but it already had the 20 doorways leading to the 'chapels' which housed the numerous divinities installed by Jayavarman VII in various towns of the empire. It should be noted, furthermore, that a succession of later embankments are an added obstacle to establishing a chronology.

No firm date for Bayon is available. It is known that, in general, the god was enshrined as soon as the infrastructure allowed, and that the superstructure was only built after his installation. The towers carved with faces can already provide a clue for dating, since this marvellous innovation had not yet occurred when Ta Prohm and Preah Khan were built. The deities were installed at Preah Khan in 1191, so it is probable that the invention of the towers carved with faces occurred around 1200 AD, and the building of the temple of Bayon, at least as far as its upper structure is concerned, had not commenced much before this date, which is not, after all, very long before Jayavarman's death. As to the dates of the various subsequent modifications, it is generally considered that they followed each other at very short intervals, but this author proposes a different 'long-term' hypothesis, which would extend the period of construction to about a century.

Opposite: Battle scene in which the Khmers defeat the Cham, southern outer gallery.

Below: Market traders from the southern outer gallery.

*Opposite: Mounted Chinese soldier in the Khmer army,
eastern outer gallery.*

Dancing apsaras *on the columns of the outer gallery.*

Overleaf: Central towers, Bayon.

A game of polo carved on the walls of the Elephant Terrace.

Above: Aerial view showing the Royal Square with the Prasats Suor Prat in the foreground.

THE RECONSTRUCTION OF THE ROYAL PALACE AND ENVIRONS

It has already been noted that Jayavarman VII took up residence in the compound of the old royal palace of Suryavarman I and his successors. He evidently needed to restore and reconstruct its buildings, but all that remains of this work are a few scattered tiles. He is widely credited with certain major works which are more likely to be attributable to Jayavarman VIII; in particular the remodelling of the 'big tank'. The more accurate history of the palace will only emerge when the current excavation project is completed. A major stele with a poem in Sanskrit, praising a deceased wife of Jayavarman VII who must have had a shrine close by, also reveals that the king did not abandon the old temple of Phimeanakas, despite its being dedicated to Shiva.

The most striking visible evidence of the king's presence at the royal palace is the sumptuous manner in which he embellished the square which lies before it to the east. He first built the famous 'Elephant Terrace', which partly masks the former eastern entrance pavilion to the palace, and extends that of Bapuon temple to the north. More than 300 metres long, it derives its name from the frieze of elephants in hunting scenes. The very recent discovery of lead tiles behind the terrace, provides a new insight into its function. The Chinese 'diplomat' Zhou Daguan recorded that "the tiles of the king's main apartments are of lead". It is thus legitimate to speculate that the Elephant Terrace was the foundation mass for the royal reception rooms, and not, as has been asserted, for lightweight buildings used on festive occasions. It would also have been where the king appeared before his people when performances were organised in the royal square on feast days. The northern part of the terrace was remodelled several times. In its second stage the wall was adorned with two fine five-headed horses, according to a legend which remains obscure. The chronology of these transformations remains to be determined.

Opposite the terrace, and to close off the square as it were, there is the line of twelve Prasats Suor Prat in laterite and sandstone: the Khmers call them 'the towers of the rope dancers', but their function remains unknown. The towers are actually rather roughly constructed, and probably do not date from Jayavarman VII's time, but more likely from that of one of his immediate successors.

North of the Elephant Terrace there is the 'Terrace of the Leper King'. It derives its name from a legendary king whom the Khmers thought they recognised in the statue on top of the terrace, but which is in fact a statue of Yama, the god of the Underworld. The site is supposed to be that of the royal cremations. The sides of the terrace are magnificently carved with six or seven rows of a multitude of characters; gods or spirits with swords, and charming goddesses, the bottom row being filled with a variety of marine creatures. When the wall was being uncovered, it was discovered that it was flanked by another row of sculptures, two metres behind, the gap between

Elephants flanking one of the projecting staircases of the Elephant Terrace.

The 'House of Fire' next to the east entrance of Ta Prohm.

them filled with laterite blocks. Thus there is evidence of yet another remodelling, its aim being simply to enlarge the surface area of the terrace. The relief friezes were subsequently extended northwards, in a project which was never fully completed.

THE 'HOUSES OF FIRE'

The Preah Khan temple inscription mentions the existence of 121 'Houses of Fire' which seem to have been placed at regular intervals along several of the main roads of the Khmer empire. It was deduced, somewhat hastily, that these 'houses' were *dharmasala*, or resting-places for travellers. Common in Indian civilisation, recently they could be frequently seen and indeed put to practical use in the villages of Cambodia. But the 'Houses of Fire' were in fact sandstone shrines, and can plausibly be identified as a specific type of building, corresponding to a series of edifices which were composed of a long hall with a tower to the west and a forepart to the east, with light entering through windows which all open southwards. Moreover, they were not an invention of Jayavarman VII, since a one is attested in the reign of Suryavarman I, in the first half of the eleventh century. It is not known what type of ceremony was held in them, but the inscriptions indicate that fire had an important role in Khmer temples, and had its own guardians. The relief friezes of Angkor Wat and Bayon depict

Chapel of the 'hospital' of Ta Muen Toch on the Thai-Cambodian border.

'fire arches' in the middle of the marching armies, and it is possible that these shrines were staging posts where these arches could be stored.

Another intriguing fact revealed briefly in the inscription, is the geographical siting of these 'houses'. They were overwhelmingly in the northern part of the empire, and it is strange why there were so few in the south, especially bearing in mind Jayavarman's preoccupation with Champa, which it seems he yearned to annex. Perhaps it was a matter of building the roads to get there in the first place.

THE HOSPITALS

The Ta Prohm inscription provides information that there existed 102 'hospitals' or *arogyasala* (literally 'houses for the sick') in the empire. Although it is not certain that Jayavarman VII should be credited with their introduction, as definite traces of similar establishments, although rare, go back to the reign of Yashovarman I, it is clear that he made special efforts to organise these 'hospitals' and to contribute to their running.

It is fortunate that almost twenty steles, each containing a long poem in Sanskrit, have been found, with their main content being a kind of set of 'rules' for the hospitals. A fairly clear idea of how they worked can thus be formed. What is not apparent, however, is whether they were true hospitals with in-patients, or merely dispensaries. As usual, the steles are primarily religious documents intended mainly for the gods – in this case especially Bhaishajyaguru, the Buddha of healing – residing in the shrine which was a compulsory element of such foundations. Thus the 'rules' served to remind the god of the king's pious actions. It is in the section devoted to the praise of the king, which is actually quite short, that this beautiful verse occurs:

"The ills of men's bodies became for him ills of the soul and thus even more afflicting, since it is the suffering of their subjects which makes the suffering of kings, and not their own sufferings."

It has often been affirmed that this text bears witness to the king's immense Buddhist compassion, but this is far from the case. It is simply the expression of the reality of kingship in the Indian world: the king literally 'is' his kingdom, and it is logical that he should feel in himself the slightest unease which might occur.

A study of these poems reveals the following. In the first place, there were four categories of hospitals. The first group included only the four establishments sited not far from the capital gates, of which two can easily be seen and are quite well preserved: Ta Prohm Kel, almost opposite Angkor Wat to the south, and the 'Chapel of the hospital' which stands near Ta Keo temple, to its east. These were clearly the most important, with the king assuming full responsibility for the upkeep of their gods, including a permanent staff of around 200. The second category is poorly documented, as only a single stele has been found – in the town of Phimai. They were foundations of almost equal importance to those in the first category, but the king did not assume the expenses of their deities. The third and fourth categories only differ in the number of staff employed in them: 98 in the former, and only 50 in the latter.

The most important information recorded in these hospital steles is that the king contributed to the support of the sick by making a donation, three times a year, of a list of medicines. The actual amounts were quite small, and thus of merely symbolic value. Only 36 items were included, almost all have been identified. These must have constituted a tiny proportion of the Khmer pharmacopoeia, suggesting the selection itself was symbolic. A pharmacological study of Jayavarman's list would undoubtedly be of the greatest interest for our knowledge of the medical practice of the time.

It is certain that Jayavarman VII was the greatest of all the Khmer kingly architects. It is also clear, however, that far too many projects have been attributed to him. While he initiated a large number of shrines, it is virtually certain that he never completed a single one, at least in the form we see today. Whatever the truth of the matter, King Jayavarman VII will have achieved immortality through his architectural feats which, far from bearing witness to his megalomania, as has too often been asserted, are proof of his immense and profound piety. This is indeed the salient feature of the admirable statues which show him in meditation before the Buddha.

Below: Ruler with consorts from the inner bas-relief of the Terrace of the Leper King.

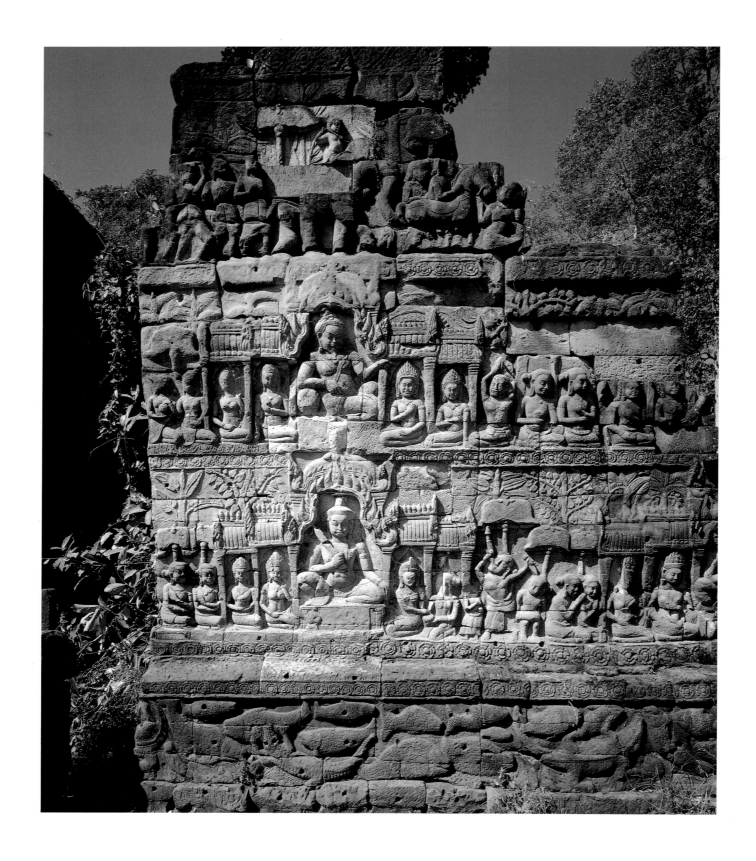

Chapter eight
The 13th Century and After

Over the years a curious association has developed between the figure of the 'leper king', which belongs to ancient legend, and King Jayavarman VII. A French doctor thought he had indeed discerned the onset of this terrible disease on the hands of a royal personage portrayed on the relief frieze of Bayon which recounts the famous legend, and which dates from the end of the thirteenth century. It can well be imagined that this diagnosis has given rise to a good deal of speculation, including the idea that it was the king's leprosy which incited him to found the hospitals! None of this is soundly based. The renowned statue of the 'leper king' which was until recently on the terrace which bears its name, in fact represents the divine judge of the underworld, Yama, and the signs of his leprosy are nothing more than lichen. The statue is by no means a masterpiece; its date is much later than the reign of Jayavarman VII, and is probably contemporary with the fourteenth century inscription engraved on its base.

After 1200 AD almost nothing is known of the life of Jayavarman VII; not even the date of his death. George Cœdès places it in the year 1220 but on rather flimsy evidence. The great king could well have passed away before then; one inscription mentions 1206 as being still within the reign, and another alludes to him in connection with a date which reads uncertainly as regards the tens, but which might correspond to 1214.

Statue of Yama, God of Death, commonly called the 'Leper King'.

Opposite: The entrance pavilion of Preah Palilay, Angkor Thom.

Face tower over the entrance to Ta Prohm's outer enclosure added after Jayavarman VII.

INDRAVARMAN II

Jayavarman's successor was Indravarman II. Nothing is known of his reign nor indeed of the circumstances of the king's accession to the throne. He died in 1243, which prompts the guess that the date of his birth was around 1180. He could thus have been Jayavarman VII's son, but by a queen whose name remains unknown. It is probable that the lack of documentation on this reign of at least twenty-five years is due in large part to the systematic destruction carried out by his successor.

There is every reason to believe that Indravarman, a Buddhist like Jayavarman VII, pursued his projects, and therefore he should probably be credited with a substantial proportion of the achievements which have traditionally been attributed wholesale to the previous reign. It is indeed quite permissible to speculate as to which of the two reigns witnessed the invention of the towers carved with faces. The chronology of art history is insecurely based on an almost non-existent chronology of historical events, and becomes even harder to establish as new monuments become rarer from the thirteenth century onwards. The frenzy of anti-Buddhist destruction in the succeeding reign would indicate that the Buddhist art of Bayon is largely attributable to the reigns of Jayavarman VII and his successor, as there was a subsequent return to Hinduist art, often imitating that of Angkor Wat.

The twelve towers – The Prasats Suor Prat – closing off the royal square of Angkor Thom to the east can fairly convincingly be attributed to the reign of Indravarman II. They are rather roughly built, using laterite and sandstone, and are aligned in two groups on terraces on either side of the royal avenue. They have an unusual feature which has aroused doubt as to their sacred nature: the cellae, which are preceded by a porch projecting to the west, all have windows on their three other sides, which is indeed highly unusual. They can only have been shrines, however, although not necessarily housing deities of Hindu origin. Zhou Daguan alludes to them as places where a sort of trial by ordeal was held: "Take the case where two men are in dispute, without its being known who is in the right or in the wrong. Opposite the royal palace there are twelve small stone towers. Each of the two men is made to sit in a tower, and each is watched over by members of his family. They remain there for one or two, or even three or four days. When they emerge, the man in the wrong has inevitably caught some disease, either afflicted by ulcers, or by catarrh or noxious fever. The man in the right has not the slightest illness. In this way they decide who is innocent and who is guilty, and they call this 'celestial judgement'." This anecdote, which may have been based on eye witness, cannot in itself explain the existence of this group of towers.

It seems that it was also in the reign of Indravarman II that the settlements around some of the Angkor temples were enclosed within high walls. They included Ta Prohm, Banteay Kdei, Ta Som and Ta Nei which were all temples or sacred compounds which had been surrounded by moats from their inception. Other towns, such as Preah Khan or Banteay Chhmar, had been enclosed within walls as part of their original design, since their moats lie outside the walled enclosure. In all probability the walls were defensive and not built without good reason. The need for them reflects a degree of insecurity – a premonition perhaps of the reign of Jayavarman VIII.

The northern Prasats Suor Prat and North Khleang in the north-east corner of the Royal Square.

STATE HINDUISM RETURNS: JAYAVARMAN VIII

While the date of Indravarman's death is known, there is no precise date for the accession to the throne of his successor, Jayavarman VIII. Although, as usual, there is no information on what actually happened, the radical religious change from one reign to the next seems to have been so ferocious that it is not difficult to guess that the interregnum was accompanied by a degree of violence and could even have lasted several years.

It is a fact that Jayavarman VIII stands out, in contrast to his predecessors, not only as a Hinduist king but also as a fierce opponent of Buddhism, and this is what seems to this author to be the most significant feature of his reign. If the

circumstances had been different he would doubtless have changed the site of his capital as many of his predecessors had done, if only to build an appropriate state temple. But he does not appear to have wished to do this, preferring instead to retain the excellent degree of protection which was already available at Angkor Thom. Within the existing layout, he declined the option of demolishing the former temple and replacing it with a new one, but instead embarked on a transformation of the central shrine of Bayon, as has already been noted, and replaced its Buddha statue with one of the god Harihara. It was then that the image of Buddha which had been enshrined by Jayavarman VII was smashed to pieces and thrown into the 'central well'. This 3.6 metre statue was found, and was restored and solemnly installed in 1935 on a nearby terrace. It is likely that at the same time Jayavarman VIII ordered the demolition of the sixteen chapels on the first level of Bayon, and their stones could even have been used to build the new angles of the second cruciform enclosure. He also walled up the doorways which opened from the chapels into the exterior galleries of relief friezes. The way was then clear for him to carve the reliefs on the interior gallery of Bayon, with their striking Hindu subjects, both Shivaite and Vishnuite. The scenes they depict have by no means all been identified but they include many themes beloved by the Khmers and often occurring in other monuments; for example the Churning of the Sea of Milk, and episodes from the great Indian epics, the *Mahabharata* and the *Ramayana*. On the way around the gallery the visitor can even find an illustration of the legend of the leper King, as the Royal chronicles recount it to this day. There is also a scene showing the building of a temple.

In addition, Jayavarman destroyed or chopped up all the Buddha images, of which very few survived. The importance of this act has been underestimated until now, and curiously was confined to Angkor, as though the royal prerogative was not strong enough to impose it elsewhere. It was, however, a considerable undertaking, when one realises that every single Buddha image carved in relief on the combs of the temple walls, at Ta Prohm, Preah Khan, Banteay Kdei, etc, estimated to total tens of thousands, was systematically destroyed at that time. Add to this the internal ornamentation and the ritual objects, which were even more significant. It is likely that the very fine bronze statues of Buddha discovered in large jars in 1968 when Siem Reap airport was being enlarged were hidden at that time, rather than during the alleged Thai invasions of subsequent centuries. While all this was going on, the Buddhas carved on the temple pillars were being re-carved rather inelegantly as Hindu ascetics.

The Prasats Chrung seem to be typical examples of the activity of Jayavarman VIII. As their name indicates, they were located at the four corners of the city of Angkor Thom, and indubitably housed protective deities which were originally Buddhist. After the death of Jayavarman VII, each of them acquired a miniature shrine

The reassembled Bayon Buddha from the central shrine.

The frieze in the 'Hall of Dancers' at Preah Khan showing that the small Buddha images have been systematically removed from their niches.

Right: The cruciform terrace in front of Angkor Wat with its later style columns.

to house a stele written by four separate authors in eulogy of the king. In the reign of Jayavarman VIII the texts of these steles were almost completely erased. The images of Buddha, especially those on the pediments, were all transformed into *linga*. It is a plausible supposition that the local guardian deities survived in their respective shrines.

Jayavarman VIII was, however, by no means a mere iconoclast, and it was probably at his behest, or at least during his reign, that modifications were undertaken at the two great Hinduist temples of Angkor Wat and Bapuon, at other less important temples such as Chau Say Tevoda and Banteay Samre, and perhaps too at the enigmatic Beng Mealea. It was arguably at that time that all these temples either acquired their causeways or their terraces built on top of cylindrical columns, or that the terraces bordered by such columns were added to them. The fact that the Khmer artists of the period occasionally reverted to the Angkor Wat style makes it all the more difficult to unravel the sequence of events.

The reign of Jayavarman VIII also saw the building of the small temple of Mangalartha, the last known monument of the Angkor period, consisting of a shrine on a high foundation mass. It was built in honour of a Brahmin scholar called Jayamangalartha, the son of one of the *gurus* of Jayavarman VII, born towards the end of the twelfth century, and who attained the remarkable age of 104. Mangalartha is in Angkor Thom, almost hidden between the two eastern causeways, and the images of its gods were 'brought to life' on Thursday 28 April 1295, at about 8.45 a.m.

Jayavarman VIII also commissioned the second phase of the terrace of the Leper King, with its accompanying images of Shiva, and the north stairway of the Elephant terrace. Some day it may indeed be realised that the famous and so far unexplained five-headed horses are not even remotely connected with Buddhism. The extension of the reliefs on the Terrace of the Leper King should be seen as part of the new project to rehabilitate the northern part of the royal square, which must also have included the building of at least several of the five Preah Pithu monuments, which have been oddly named as a group by the local people, but which do not have obvious links with each other, except those of proximity. Four of them are to the north of the Royal Square and, similar in style, should be seen as relating to Preah Palilay, but this exclusively Buddhist shrine raises a problem: if, as is sometimes claimed, it dates from the first half of the thirteenth century, how could it have escaped the assault of Jayavarman VIII? It might be better to think of it as dating from the later years of the reign of the ageing Jayavarman, who may have at last discovered the virtue of tolerance.

Jayavarman VIII had a lengthy reign of around 50 years. Although all that is visible today bears witness to his religious activities, it is highly likely that his accession was determined by political causes. There are strong indications that he belonged to a lineage which had been dispossessed by Jayavarman VII. His zeal in destroying any testimony to the previous reigns is remarkable. There is a defaced inscription in Bayon temple on which the name of a 'Jayavarman' can still be deciphered, and this could only be Jayavarman VII. Jayavarman VIII doubtless destroyed much more written evidence, as for example the steles of the Prasat Chrung.

A result of late 13th century iconoclasm, a Buddha image on a pediment at Neak Pean has been crudely recarved as a linga.

Left: On the upper level of Angkor Wat, the round columns of the projecting porch were brought here from the cruciform terrace in the 16th century.

The precious stele of Phimeanakas has also been found. It had been deliberately smashed and lay beneath an embankment several metres deep, which indicates, incidentally, that its burial was the work of Jayavarman VIII. This in turn gives rise to the thought that it was Jayavarman, too, who commissioned the remodelling of the 'Great Pond', which measured 125 metres by 45, and was embellished with rows of stone steps, the last three being finely sculpted with a frieze of more or less fanciful fish, and above it a row of *naga*, while the top row was adorned with pairs of *garuda*. To the south, a wall was built to support a terrace from which the king could watch the festivals which would have been staged on the waters of the pond.

It was during the reign of Jayavarman VIII that the Thais of the northern region of present-day Thailand, who had begun to chafe at the bit in the first half of the thirteenth century, consolidated their kingdoms; at Sukhothai to the detriment of the Khmers, and at Chiang Mai to the detriment of a Mon dynasty. From then on, they would often be in conflict, with varying degrees of success, with the Khmer empire until their final victory at the end of the sixteenth century. At the same time the country of Lavo (today's Lopburi) appears to have achieved independence.

A significant event of the final years of the reign was the arrival in South-East Asia of Kublai Khan's Mongols. One of his hordes, setting out from Champa, may have mounted an unsuccessful attack on Cambodia in 1283. Nevertheless the king decided that it was prudent, after all, to pay tribute to the great Khan in 1285 and 1292.

The reassembled stele of Phimeanakas which was excavated from beneath a deep embankment.

Detail of bas-reliefs around the Great Pond of the Royal Palace. Although the pond is earlier the carvings date to the time of Jayavarman VIII.

Figure, hidden terrace, Elephant Terrace, since vandalised.

Left: Five-headed horse, in deep relief, possibly from a Hindu legend, hidden by a later wall, Elephant Terrace.

Ruins of the fourth temple (right) and third temple (below) at Preah Pithu. The five temples that make up this group were built at different times.

The remodelled pond and bas-reliefs probably executed by Jayavarman VIII in the Royal Enclosure, north of Phimeanakas.

A Chinese Emissary At Angkor

Jayavarman was forced to abdicate in 1295 under pressure from his son-in-law, who assumed power under the name of Srindravarman. Not long after this, in 1296 or 1297, an ambassador from China arrived in Angkor bringing in his retinue Zhou Daguan who was the author of a famous and remarkably lively report *Memoirs on the Customs of Cambodia*, which has been widely consulted by students of the ancient Khmers. His account reveals that the changing of kings could have been more violent than the inscriptions suggest: "The new prince, he writes, is the son-in-law of the former sovereign. His former duty was to be in command of the army. The father-in-law loved his daughter, and the daughter stole the golden sword from him and took it to her husband. Consequently the son-and-heir was deprived of the succession. He plotted to raise troops, but the new prince discovered the plot, cut off his toes, and locked him in a dark room."

The golden sword mentioned here is doubtless the famous Preah Khan, the palladium of the empire, a copy of which was until recent times carefully guarded by the Brahmins of the royal palace of Phnom Penh.

It is largely thanks to Zhou Daguan that the town of Angkor Thom can assume a degree of liveliness for the present-day reader. The Chinese writer tells us in fact that he was an eye-witness of royal ceremonies which he describes at some length:

"When the prince appears, there are troops at the head of his escort, followed by standard-bearers, flag-bearers and musicians. Palace maidens, three to five hundred in number, in floral-patterned clothes and with flowers in their coiled-up hair, carry candles in their hands and themselves make up a separate troupe. Even in full daylight their candles are lit. Next come palace maidens carrying the gold and silver royal utensils and the whole series of ornaments, all wrought in very distinctive styles whose use is unknown to me. Then come palace maidens holding in their hands a lance and a shield, and who are the private palace guards: they too form a separate troupe. After them come goat-carts and horse-carts, all bedecked with gold. The ministers and princes are all on elephant back; from afar their innumerable red parasols can be seen. After them come the wives and concubines of the king in palanquins, in carts, on horseback or on elephant back; they have surely more than a hundred parasols spangled with gold. Behind them at last comes the king, standing on the back of an elephant and holding in his hand the precious sword. The tusks of the elephant are sheathed in gold. There are more than twenty white parasols spangled with gold and with gold handles. Numerous elephants crowd around him and there is a further detachment of troops to guard him . . . One can thus see that while they are a kingdom of barbarians, these people have not forgotten what it is to be a prince."

There are many details, however, which show that this account is not always worthy of the blind confidence which has often been accorded to it. There was a Chinese colony at Angkor among whom Zhou Daguan found his main sources. It is more often the tales peddled by this group, rather than his own eye-witness experiences, which he recounts, having accepted their stories unreservedly, since they concerned these 'barbarians'.

Thus he tells of the following marvel: "In the town, near the Eastern gate, there was a barbarian who fornicated with his younger sister. Their skin and their flesh fused together without becoming detached and, after three days without food, the two of them died. My 'fellow-countryman' Mr Sie, who has spent thirty-five years in this country, asserts that he has seen such a case happen twice. If this is so, it shows that the people of this country know how to use the supernatural power of the holy Buddha".

In the same way, there has been a strangely uncritical acceptance of the chapter which recounts the nights of the king at the summit of Phimeanakas, which is undoubtedly based on a fanciful legend: "The natives all claim that in the tower there is a genie which is a nine-headed serpent and is the master of all the land of the kingdom. Each night it appears in the shape of a woman. It is with her that the sovereign sleeps first and has congress." Here it is easy to detect the legend which relates that Soma was the daughter of the King of the *Nagas* of that region. Additionally it should be noted that the "master of all the land of the kingdom" is

King Suryavarman II riding his elephants in procession, Historical Gallery of bas-reliefs, Angkor Wat.

Opposite: Provincial troops precede the King in procession, Historical Gallery of bas-reliefs, Angkor Wat.

none other than the *Devaraja*, thus opening the door to a whole host of legends in this connection.

It has long been observed that Zhou Daguan made some glaring errors about the geography of the capital, especially concerning the *baray*. It is obvious that he had no intention of writing a sort of 'tourist's guide': on the contrary, his account is much more like a report on the economic significance of the country. Nevertheless the document is unique for its abundance of lively vignettes on every subject, both in the capital and in the hinterland, although it is occasionally necessary to be more rigorous than Zhou was, about the quality of the information he received. Even the element of fantasy in his stories is not without value, as it gives an idea of the living environment of the Khmers, and also of the way they were perceived by foreigners.

One last point of interest is that Zhou Daguan calls Angkor Wat "the tomb of Lou Pan". Lou Pan was an ancient, legendary Chinese artisan, and it seems that even at this early time, the Khmers had confused Vishnuloka, which was the posthumous name of King Suryavarman II, the builder of the temple, and Vishvakarman, the divine builder, who is sometimes credited with the fashioning of Angkor Wat. It was the latter name which the Chinese remembered, and they related it to the one they were familiar with in their own legends. For present-day scholars the name would have been as impenetrable as those of Funan or Chenla, had they not had a knowledge of Khmer legend to unravel the mystery.

Srindravarman, who had married a daughter of Jayavarman VIII, was a descendant of the line of Sreshthapura, which meant he was related to Jayavarman VII. He was a Buddhist, and this should have made him an opponent of his father-in-law, but his faith was not exactly that of Jayavarman VII. In fact he bequeathed the first inscription in Pali in Cambodia, which thus clearly marks the official espousal of Theravada Buddhism, which arrived in Cambodia from Ceylon, probably under the influence of the Thai kingdoms. It may have been during Srindravarman's reign that some of the shrines of Ta Prohm came back into service. They had probably been abandoned for some while, but at that time various projects were implemented to raise the level of their interior courtyards. In general, this was low-grade work which could only have been carried out by individual initiative, a supposition which is borne out by the inscriptions which were engraved on them at the same time. Apart from the other information, the Pali inscription bears the date of 1309, two years after the abdication of Srindravarman in favour of a prince of his own line, known by the name of Srindrajayavarman, who reigned for 22 years without leaving any documented traces. In 1327, the next king, Jayavarman Paramesvara, acceded to the throne. His name is revealed in the very last Sanskrit inscription discovered at Angkor, not far from the north-east corner of the moat of Angkor Wat, and actually commissioned by a Brahmin ascetic of Hindu origin. Of this king, neither his achievements nor the date of his death are known.

Although there are no more inscriptions for a period of more than two centuries, there are significant accounts which give an idea of the splendour of Angkor in the fourteenth century. The Chinese chronicler, Zhao Rugua still speaks in 1349 of "rich and noble Cambodia", as had Zhou Daguan half a century earlier, after giving a wonderful description of his visit. While the wooden pagodas which replaced the temples have vanished, their foundation masses have survived, and are what are now called the 'Buddhist terraces'. There have long been records of over 60 of them in the town of Angkor Thom alone, and there is nothing to suggest that these shrines were in any way less sumptuous than those which appeared later in Cambodia and Thailand. A study of the way these terraces were laid out could also provide precious information on how the town might have looked at that time. At this period several shrines in Angkor Thom underwent more transformations, and further reliefs were carved to the north of the Elephant Terrace, on the walls of the so-called 'Sanctuary X' at Preah Pithu, and in the monument only known by its inventory number (486), which is built over a tenth century shrine.

It was probably also in the fourteenth century that the four doorways of the central shrine of Angkor Wat were walled up, and the stones used for this were sculpted with large standing Buddha figures, thus transforming the shrine into a kind of *stupa* which has remained in worship ever since.

The very few subsequent historical documents available, mainly consist of the various versions of the Royal Chronicles. It is often forgotten, however, that these were only written down from the beginning of the nineteenth century onwards, and that they should not be read without a good measure of critical judgement. They all agree on the fact that the Khmer King Chau Ponhea Yat 'abandoned' Angkor, though they give a wide range of dates, from 1377 to 1508. He did so after the final attack by the Thais, fleeing to take up residence in the south: first at Basan in the province of Srei Santhor, then at Phnom Penh, and finally at Longvek. Good arguments have been advanced to cast doubt on this 'abandonment' of Angkor, and it is not merely because the Chronicles are the only 'historical' documents that are available that they should be considered as definitively authoritative. The American scholar Michael Vickery has carried out intensive research which shows that it is in fact difficult to give them any credence when they deal with this period of Khmer history. He is quite right to conclude that it would be surprising if these texts, which recount Khmer history from its beginnings to the fifteenth century and are unanimously considered to be legendary, could miraculously become 'historical' at the precise moment when the inscriptions almost entirely vanish. The writers of the Chronicles were working in the nineteenth century on the basis of documents which have never been published, and they tried to reconstruct a coherent Khmer history. They had no qualms about rewriting various chapters when the source material was too scarce, which was often the case over the whole period.

Whatever the truth of the matter, it is very doubtful that the kings of Angkor fled from their capital because of Thai onslaughts, (they were in any case fewer than claimed in the Chronicles) in order to take up residence in Phnom Penh. It is at least as credible that, in fact, the king of Angkor never 'abandoned' the city, but that a descendant from a different royal lineage, or perhaps from another branch of the family which reigned at Angkor, installed himself as a rival in the Phnom Penh region which was growing in economic importance because of the burgeoning Chinese trading activity in South-East Asia. In contrast to the various theories advanced over the years with more or less plausibility, Michael Vickery's hypothesis is well worth considering, namely that it was the growing economic importance of Phnom Penh as a port, and – even more – that of Ayutthaya, capital of Siam, which endangered the power of Angkor and finally led to its downfall. It follows from this, that – contrary to received opinion – the 'restoration of Angkor Wat' may well have had nothing to do with the kings of Longvek, Satha, or elsewhere. The two kings who left inscriptions at

Angkor in the second half of the sixteenth century do not appear to have had links with the kings of Longvek: could they not instead have been the last, or among the last, kings of Angkor? There is also the puzzle as to why any Khmer king should wish to take up residence afresh, and provisionally, at Angkor. There is absolutely no evidence for this either in the inscriptions or in the Royal Chronicles.

THE FIRST DISCOVERY OF ANGKOR BY WESTERNERS

"Just about the years 1550 or 1551, as the king of Camboja set off to hunt elephant in the thickest forests which exist in the whole Kingdom, his beaters who were thrashing their way through the bush came upon some imposing buildings overgrown inside by vegetation so exuberant that they could not cut it down to gain access. When this was reported to the king, he went to the place and saw the extent and the height of the outer walls. As he wished to see what was inside, he immediately ordered that the scrub be all cut down and burned."

This is what the official chronicler of the Portuguese Indies, Diogo do Couto, wrote in the second half of the sixteenth century in what purports to be a report on Angkor. According to him and other travellers, the Khmers 'discovered' their former capital around the year 1550. This 'discovery', recounted in more or less detail in a good number of Spanish and Portuguese accounts of the period, is often accompanied by the assertion that the Khmers were ignorant of anything which related to the origin of the ruins. For example, one of them writes:

"It is an astonishing fact that none of the natives of this kingdom can survive there, and thus the place is inhabited only by wild and savage beasts. The tradition of these gentiles is that the city was built be foreigners".

The Spaniards and the Portuguese thus began to speculate as to who had been the real builder of Angkor, and came up with the most astonishing names, such as Alexander or Trajan. They also imagined that it was the embodiment of "the figmentary city of Plato's Atlantis, or even that of his Republic". It is certain that these preposterous theories did not originate with the Khmers themselves; but they could not have been dreamt up unless the Khmers had insisted that they knew nothing of their past, and even less about the ruins.

Quite evidently, this was not the case, as there are inscriptions engraved in stone at approximately the same period which contradict it. In fact it was around the middle of the sixteenth century that at least one Khmer king took an interest in Angkor Wat. Between 1546 and 1564, a king whose name remains obscure, ordered the carving of some six hundred square metres of relief friezes on the east side of the north gallery and the north side of the east gallery which had remained blank since the twelfth

Devata *on the central sanctuary of Bakheng defaced with bullet holes. The temple's hill-top location gave it strategic importance during the civil war, and it was occupied in succession by the Khmer Rouge and the Vietnamese Army.*

century, when the original artists had presumably run out of time to complete them. These sixteenth-century additions are clearly influenced by the art of Ayutthaya.

Moreover, at some time before 1577, King Tribhuvanadityavarman, who was probably the son of the king referred to above, ordered "the restoration of Brah Bisnulok of ancient Cambodia to its real former state . . . he restored the great temple of Brah Bisnulok, the enclosure wall stone by stone; he reconstructed the nine towers of the temple and embellished them by sheathing them in gold." In the same text the same king wishes that his son, the young prince, might govern Cambodia "like the former lineage of kings which built the great capital Indrapattha and the majestic Vishnuloka as well as all strongholds within the Cambodian territory". It is clear from this that the Khmer kings still claimed their place as successors to the kings of Angkor, and it should be noted in passing that as early as this period at least, the Sanskrit word *mahanagara* is used to designate Angkor Thom, which is its exact translation in the Khmer language.

The workmanship was sometimes clumsy, for example when round columns were taken from the base of a temple and used on foreparts looking out over the courtyards at its summit, where they do not match with others which have a square section (see page 283). Some magnificent wooden statues may date from this period, including the justly famous 'worshipper' from Angkor Wat. The fine 'modern' *devata* which adorn the pillars of the third storey are probably more recent.

Angkor Wat was not the only focus of interest for these kings. They also had a taste for monumental statuary, for example the drafted stone Buddha at Tep Pranam, and the reclining Buddha at Bapuon which re-utilises the whole length of the western gallery of the third enclosure and the nearby stones. The seated Buddha at Phnom Bakheng would have been colossal if it had been completed, but only the lotus pedestal and the legs seem to have been actually built. Nearby, however, in the centre of the broad eastern avenue, a Buddha footprint was carved into the rock, and to this day is still venerated. One final point worthy of note is the stele in Arabic script which is tentatively dated to the seventeenth century, in the reign of an 'apostate' king who had married a Muslim Cham princess.

Phnom Kulen also regained its place (if it had ever been lost) as a major religious centre, and the great reclining Buddha was carved into the rock at Preah Thom. The nearby caves sheltered hermits, as they had done in ancient times.

AN UPSURGE IN THE ECONOMY

The schemes to restore and further decorate Angkor Wat and other temples could not have been undertaken without a degree of economic prosperity, to which a number of mainly hydrological projects bear witness. Diogo do Couto relates that the canal system in Angkor Thom was still serviceable, which proves that it had been maintained at least until the latter part of the sixteenth century. Moreover, due to a combination of circumstances, arising from the presence to the east of the East Baray of the wall built by Jayaviravarman which connects with the wall built for the town of Jayavarman VII, plus the West Baray to the west, Angkor had been effectively closed off to the north by a 20 kilometre dam which inevitably brought about serious flooding during the rainy season. It was probably during this period that the decision was taken to breach the old wall of Jayaviravarman to allow the Siem Reap river to flow through it. The river may well have been diverted in former times to connect with the canals which irrigated the whole region north of the East Baray, but thenceforth was to run along a former waterway which had been dug between the *baray* and Angkor Thom. A bridge was built over it, – Spean Thma – ('stone bridge'), from blocks of sandstone, many of which are carved. At least some of these stones were salvaged from a post-Angkor temple, which gives an indication of the age of the bridge. It is quite noticeable that at this spot the river does not quietly follow the bed of the former canal, designed for a much smaller volume of water than it now had to cope with. Instead, it veered from the cobbled bed which had been laid down for it under the piers of the bridge, and eroded a new deep channel to the east.

ANGKOR WAT: A SIXTEENTH CENTURY PILGRIMAGE ENTRE

Quite apart from the involvement of the Khmer kings at Angkor Wat, the temple seems to have been renowned as a holy place in the sixteenth century, another fact of which the Spaniards and the Portuguese were evidently unaware. We know that it was famous in far-away places under the name of Jetavana, an important site mentioned in the stories of the life of Buddha, near Sravasti in India. A ground plan of the temple, drawn by a Japanese merchant in the seventeenth century, has also come to light. He is assumed to have travelled there from Ayutthaya, attracted by the fame of Angkor Wat, and the legend on the drawing shows that the merchant thought he was actually in India!

The renown of the temple seems to have gradually faded over time, but there is no reason to believe that Angkor Wat was ever forgotten. A later reference shows on the contrary the great importance it had retained in the minds of the Khmers. At a

17-18th century Buddha image in wood from the post-Angkor period.

Foreigners on the main causeway of Angkor Wat in the 1920s.

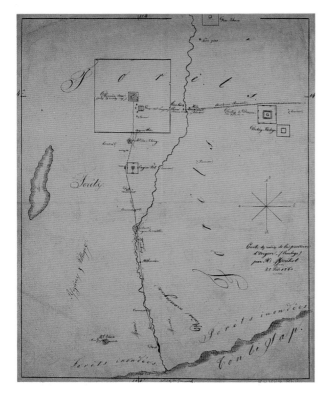

Map drawn by Henri Mouhot. (Photo: © Royal Geographical Society)

Opposite: The now overgrown inner enclosure of Banteay Chhmar, with the remains of the face tower.

Overleaf
South-west corner of Ta Prohm's enclosure.

particularly dark period of Khmer history, Queen Ang Mei, a prisoner of the Vietnamese around 1840, had had the profile of the three famous towers of Angkor Wat engraved on her personal seal.

THE SECOND DISCOVERY OF ANGKOR BY THE WEST

The West was quite unaware of the Khmer ruins, as no-one had noticed the reports the Spaniards and the Portuguese had written about their expeditions. There are no references to these in the accounts written by the Frenchmen who arrived in Ayutthaya at the end of the seventeenth century.

In fact the first European to report the existence of the monuments of Angkor was not the famous botanist Henri Mouhot, as has often been asserted, but a French missionary, Father Bouillevaux, who had settled in Battambang, which at the time was under Thai jurisdiction. In his memoirs he expresses some disgust at having been upstaged in this way, and proves that he had a good knowledge of the other visitors to Angkor who had been there before him. In his book published in 1874, he writes: "Before I proceed, I wish to register my protest against a certain system of exaggeration and charlatanism. It is claimed that in Cambodia and elsewhere some valuable discoveries have been made. Most of these fine discoveries have long been known. Thus for example the pagoda of Angcor and the ruins of Angcor Thom were not found by Mouhot, as has been claimed, for the good reason that they never were forgotten nor lost. The missionaries knew of them, and have given succinct accounts of them. Portuguese travellers in the sixteenth century had visited them, and indeed certain Chinese chroniclers in the thirteenth century mention them more or less clearly in their accounts. Mouhot saw Angcor after a number of others, and in particular after me, but his expedition attracted much publicity and he introduced this country to many readers. The officers of the Mekong expedition, in particular Monsieur de Lagree, have studied the monuments intensively and they provide interesting descriptions of them. This is the truth . . . But let us not exaggerate."

It was indeed Father Bouillevaux, five years before the visit of Mouhot, who revealed the existence of the ruins, which in fact had not greatly excited him. But to give him his rightful credit, the role of Henri Mouhot, whose explorations lasted from 1858 until his death in 1861, was much more important than that of the missionary.

From that time on, explorers and archaeologists worked tirelessly on the monuments, trying to wrest from them the secrets of the civilisation which had created them. Much more remains to be done, but great progress has been made, and it is hoped that, after the appalling cataclysm suffered by the Khmer, all and sundry will be able to see the marvels of Angkor, and witness the renaissance of the Khmer people.

The Photography

It had long been an ambition of mine to photograph Angkor. I had already started with Khmer temples in Thailand for what eventually became another book, *Palaces of the Gods,* and this only made me more enthusiastic to go to Cambodia. As a visual experience, the site is unique. Nowhere else does great architecture and tropical forest coincide, and if Angkor was never completely abandoned and forgotten, it is certainly the Lost City of our imagination. All the elements are present, and they are largely visual: the grandiose scale of everything, from the temples as models of the universe to the extent of the bas-reliefs; the artistry of the carving; the resistance of the stone and its ability to survive the centuries; and the envelopment by the forest. More than this, a romantic bonus is the obsessive creation of the giant stone faces by Jayavarman VII. If anything comes close to Shelley's Ozymandias, it is these, with the insinuating roots of immense trees taking the place of lone and level sands.

Naturally, it was all the more attractive for being at the time virtually closed, as it had been for almost two decades, since the North Vietnamese Army and the Khmer Rouge had taken the temples during the war. It meant, among other things, that I could work on ground that had not already been thoroughly covered by other photographers. All the important photography, from John Thomson onwards, had been in black-and-white, and no major book in colour had ever been attempted. Nevertheless, the problems of actually getting there were at the time formidable. Cambodia had virtually no consular representation, and the only means of entry was through Vietnam, itself in a xenophobic period. I was fortunate that the Smithsonian magazine agreed to an assignment; after that, with persistence and luck, I reached Angkor in the rainy season of 1989.

The state of tropical ruin was never more pronounced. It was remarkable how quickly the forest had started to reclaim the monuments. We had to cut our way through some, while others were completely off limits. I was supposed to wait for an armed guard before entering anywhere, but at Preah Khan one morning I started without. As I walked through the waist-high grass, there was a shout from behind. I stopped and turned. A guard was running, waving frantically. He pushed past me, and about twenty paces ahead knelt down. After a minute he signalled me on; he had disconnected the tripwire attached to a grenade. Every night the guards booby-trapped the outlying temples to catch Khmer Rouge patrols (who retaliated in like fashion).

The modern catastrophe of Cambodia was never far. The photograph that opens the chapter on Angkor Wat posed an unusual problem. For most of the big architectural shots, I used a view camera with 4x5-inch film, and one of the needs of a large-format camera in low light was a long exposure, usually some seconds. As the sun just started to reach the tower, and I was about to shoot, I saw the bubble in the camera's spirit level tremble. At almost the same instant, a boom echoed around the walls. The morning artillery barrage had begun a dozen kilometres away. To avoid the picture being shaken into a blur, I had to time the exposures between the shells being fired.

From a photographer's point of view, one of the attractive features of Khmer architecture is that two quite different scales co-exist perfectly. The best of the temples are indeed architectural triumphs, but at the same time are a canvas for exquisite carvings, these at a level of detail where the texture of the stone itself comes into play. Photographically, this means moving from one world to another. At times there seems no limit to the distances at which a temple can fill the frame-from afar, the towers of Angkor Wat are a powerful demonstration of architecture dominating the forest, while from a few inches, the hand of an *apsara* shows an equal dedication of intent.

The light, as always with buildings and landscapes, makes all the difference. At Angkor, the often complex arrangements of towers, galleries, pavilions, and the forest settings, add to the normal variety of weather and time of day to give an endless choice.

The only requirement is the patience to wait, and then work quickly to make the most of fleeting conditions. In the case of the bas-reliefs, however, the Khmer architects were clearly not beset with these aesthetic considerations. Normally it is not possible to talk of best and worst lighting, but the two greatest series of bas-reliefs at Angkor were, for one reason or another, displayed very poorly-within galleries where the light comes indirectly through a low opening opposite. Not only did this flatten the relief, but made the upper parts always too dark. Fortunately, I was able to see the Churning of the Sea of Milk at a time when the gallery roof and pillars were removed; the crisply lit details of the very fine carving may come as a surprise to anyone who knows the panel in its murky galleried setting. The absence of a gallery roof is also, of course, what helps the appreciation of the Bayon's historical bas-reliefs. As for the rest, there was no alternative but to use artificial lighting, something I prefer to do without.

Visiting and photographing Angkor is now easy and straightforward, although I admit that I miss having the temples completely to myself, as I did on the first two visits. The years since then have, in a way, been a small recapitulation of the discovery of Angkor, beginning with the clearing of the undergrowth in late 1989. In time, more and more temples were opened, the mines cleared, restoration projects resumed and new archeological work begun. Not for the first time, Angkor is in a period of recovery.

ACKNOWLEDGMENTS:

Many people helped me in the years during which these photographs were taken, but none more so than Yeang Sokhon, who guided me around the temples from the beginning, including some that were distinctly unsafe at the time. I am also indebted to Chhay Son Heng, Mme Sun Sapheun, Tim Carney, Janosz Jelen, Don Moser and Caroline Despard.

CHRONOLOGY

DATES	WORLDWIDE EVENTS	BUILDINGS	CAMBODIA EVENTS	BUILDINGS
320-c.550	Gupta empire, India	Ajanta Caves, Sanchi temples		
5th C	'Great Chronicle composed in Pali, Sri Lanka			
476	Fall of Roman Empire in West			
514			Death of Jayavarman (of Funan) and accession of Rudravarman in South Cambodia	
560	Scythian rule ends in Bactria			
563		Hagia Sophia, Constantinople		
596	St. Augustine arrives in England	First Benedictine monastery (Cantebury)		
600			Mahendravarman assumes power at Bhavapura Sambor Prei Kuk	
605	Chinese invasion of Champa			
615			Accession of Ishanavarman I	Sambor Prei Kuk, South group
618	T'ang dynasty in China			
618-1276		Dunhuang 'Caves of 1,000 Buddhas'		
622	Mohammed flees to Medina			
625-75		Mamallapuram temples, South India; Mi-Son E1 style, Champa		
628			Death of Ishanavarman and break-up of his empire	
638	Arabs capture Jerusalem Pyu capital Sri Ksetra founded	Brick stupas, Prome, Burma		

DATES	WORLDWIDE EVENTS	BUILDINGS	CAMBODIA EVENTS	BUILDINGS
655			Accession of Jayavarman I	
668-935	Unified Siller dynasty, Korea			
670				Ak Yum temple
693		Dome of Rock begun, Jerusalem		
700			Death of Jayavarman I and break-up of his empire	
708		Horyuji temple, Japan		Kompong Preah and Prei Kmeng styles
711	Arabs invade Spain			
713			Queen Jayadevi in the Angkor region	
732	Charles Martel defeats Saracens at Poitier			
c.750-825		Borobudur temple, Java		
c.750-c.1100	Pala dynasty, Eastern India	Nalanda monastery, Great Stupa of Paharpur		
785		Offa's Dyke, England		
790			Jayavarman II crowned king at Indrapura	
794		Kyoto becomes capital of Japan		
800	Charlemagne crowned Emperor	Aix-la-Chapelle, France		
802			Jayavarman II consecrated as *cakravartin*, 'universal emperor'	Kulen style
829	Egbert, first English king			
832	Sack of Pyu capital, Halin, by Nan Chao			
846	Arabs sack Rome		Jayavarman III	
867	Viking Kingdom founded York, England			

DATES	WORLDWIDE EVENTS	BUILDINGS	CAMBODIA EVENTS	BUILDINGS
875-910		Don Du'ong style, Champa		
877			Indravarman I becomes 'King of the Khmer kings'	
880				Dedication of Preah Ko temple
881				Dedication of Bakong state temple
889			Yashovarman I becomes 'King of the Khmer kings'	
893				Dedication of Lolei temple
905				Dedication of Phnom Bakheng temple
907	Collapse of T'ang dynasty			Baksei Chamkrong temple
c.915		Prambanan temple, Java First abbey, Cluny, France	Harshavarman I Ishanavarman II	
928			Jayavarman IV, king of Koh Ker, becomes 'King of the Khmer kings'	Koh Ker state temple
944			Rajendravarman, king of Bhavapura, becomes 'King of Khmer kings'	
948				Rededication of Baksei Chamkrong
950		Daigo-ji Pagoda, Kyoto		
953				Dedication of East Mebon
960-1276	Sung dynasty			
961				Dedication of Pre Rup state temple
963		First recorded London Bridge		

DATES	WORLDWIDE EVENTS	BUILDINGS	CAMBODIA EVENTS	BUILDINGS
967				Dedication of Banteay Srei
c.968			Jayavarman V, son of Rajendravarman, becomes 'King of Khmer kings'	
1000			Death of Jayavarman V	Ta Keo state temple
1001			Udayadityavarman I	
1002			Suryavarman I has himself crowned as 'King of Khmer kings' in same year as Jayaviravarman A long war ensues	
1004	Pagan, Srivijaya and Tajik Embassies to the Sung court			
1011			Final victory of Suryavarman I	Royal Palace of Angkor Thom Phimeanakas
1019-49	King Airlangga, Java			
1033-34	Muslims sack Benares			
1044-1077	King Aniruddha, Pagan			
1050			Udayadityavarman II, 'King of Khmer king'	Bapuon state temple
c.1050	Khmer invasion of Hamsavati (Pegu) Burma			
1066	Norman conquest of England			
1080			Harshavarman III, brother of his predecessr Jayavarman VI, of the Mahidharapura dynasty becomes 'King of Khmer kings'	Phimai temple
1070-1130		Canterbury and many other Norman cathedrals in England and France		
1094		Completion of St. Mark's, Venice		

Dates	Worldwide Events	Buildings	Cambodia Events	Buildings
1099	Crusades capture Jerusalem			
1113			Suryavarman II eliminates 'two' sovereigns and becomes 'King of Khmer kings'	
c.1130		Alcazar (Spain) begun		
c.1140 temple				Angkor Wat state begun
c.1150			Accession of Yashovarman II	Beng Mealea, Banteay Samre, Chau Say Tevoda, Thommanon
c.1155		Thatbyinnyu temple, Pagan		
1163		Notre-Dame, Paris		
1165			Accession of Tribhuvanadityavarman	
1170	Murder of Thomas-a-Becket, Canterbury			
1174		Leaning Tower of Pisa		
1177			Sack of Angkor by the Chams under Jaya-Indravarman IV	
1181			Jayavarman VII vanquishes Jaya-Indravarman IV and becomes 'King of Khmer kings'	Walled city of Angkor Thom, Bayon state temple, Ta Prohm temple, the hospitals
1191				Preah Khan temple
1193	Death of Saladin			
1213		Alhambra begun	c.1210 Jayavarman VII dies	
1214-1218	Genghis Khan seizes Peking and conquers Persia			
1243			Jayavarman VIII	The centre of Bayon becomes a Shiva shrine
1258	Mongols sack Baghdad			

DATES	WORLDWIDE EVENTS	BUILDINGS	CAMBODIA EVENTS	BUILDINGS
1273	Rudolf, first Hapsburg Emperor			
1276-1368	Yuan dynasty			
1283	Sukhothai kingdom, Thailand			
c.1284	Mongols capture Pagan			
1293-c.1528	Majapahit dynasty, Java			
1295				Dedication of Mangalartha temple
1296	Foundation of Chiang Mai, Thailand			
1315	Shans establish Ava, captital in Sagaing, Burma			
1309	Avignon popes	1342-1360 Papal Palace, Avignon		
1337-1453	Hundred Years wars, between France and England			
1348	The Great Plague			
1350	Foundation of Ayutthaya, Thailand			
1368-1644	Ming Dynasty			
1369		Panataram temple, Java		
1431	Death of Joan of Arc	Traditional date for conquest of Angkor by the Thais		
1453	Fall of Constantinople			
1555		Gaspar da Cruz, a Portugese Dominican, tries unsuccessfully to reside at King Ang Chan's court at Lovek		
late 16th C		First description of Angkor in Europe by Diogo do Couto		

GLOSSARY

NB: The transcription of Sanskrit and Khmer words has been kept as simple as possible, which has meant dropping the accents and diacritics normally used in scholarly books and articles.

acroter (arch. term): pinnacle or other ornament that stands on a parapet.

anastylosis (arch. term): restoration technique in which all elements of the structure are analysed, numbered and reassembled, with new materials only used where structurally necessary.

Airavata (Sanskrit): Sacred elephant and vehicle of the god Indra. One of the elephants that supports the four corners of the world.

Angkor, Nokor (Sanskrit adapted to Khmer): - from *nagara* 'capital', as in Angkor Borei (the 'capital town', south of Phnom Penh); Banteay Prei Nokor (' the fortress of the capital which was a forest'; the presumed site of Indrapura, Jayavarman II's capital); and also Prei Nokor (the 'forest capital', which is still the Khmer name for Saigon).

apsaras (Sanskrit): celestial female dancer, often promised as a reward for heroes who die in battle.

arogyasala (Sanskrit): 'house for the sick'. It is uncertain whether these were real hospitals, or merely dispensaries.

ashrama (Sanskrit): 'hermitage'. A kind of retreat house where men whose active life was over, could prepare for their next life.

asuras (Sanskrit): devilish monsters involved in fights with the *devas*.

avatar (Sanskrit): 'descent', such as that of Vishnu to earth under various forms: Rama, Krishna, or Kurma the tortoise, the pivot in the 'Churning of the Sea of Milk'.

Ba– (Khmer prefix for the modern names of temples such as Bakheng, Bayon): used for temple mountains symbolising the earth, (lit. 'father'; in contrast with *Me-* ('mother', as in Mebon – temples linked with water).

Balaha (Sanskrit): Horse from Buddhist mythology and was one of the previous incarnations of the Buddha.

banteay (Khmer): 'fortress'. Many temples have it as part of their name because of their surrounding walls.

baray (Sanskrit): pond, or reservoir.

Bhadravarman (Sanskrit): 'the (King) protected by luck'.

Bhaishajyaguru (Sanskrit): a Mahayanan Buddha considered to be the master of medecine and worshipped as such in the *arogyasala*.

Bhavavarman (Sanskrit): 'the (King) protected by Bhava' (lit. 'the life', a name for Shiva).

Bodhisattva (Sanskrit): One who is on the way to *nirvana* but delays arrival through compassion for suffering beings (lit. 'one whose essence is perfect Knowledge').

Brahma (Sanskrit, *Prohm* in Khmer): a member of the Hindu trinity, along with Shiva and Vishnu *(see below)*. Brahma's roles are various, but he is generally known as the Creator and framer of the Universe.

Buddha (Sanskrit): 'the enlightened (One)'. There have been innumerable Buddhas, of whom the last is Siddhartha Gautama (VIth century BC).

chakravartin (Sanskrit): 'he who turns the wheel (of Law)'; title taken by the emperor of India, and adopted by Jayavarman II.

deva, devata (Sanskrit): deities, with devatas being lesser deities.

Devaraja (Sanskrit): ' the god who is King'. Translation of the Khmer title *kamrateng jagat ta raja*, meaning 'the (local) divinity entrusted with governance of the kingdom'.

devata (Sanskrit): 'deity' in the most general sense of the term.

Devi (Sanskrit): One of the names of Uma, Shiva's consort.

Dharanindravarman (Sanskrit): 'the (King) protected by Indra, Lord of the Earth'.

Dvarapala (Sanskrit): 'guardian of the gate'; deities placed at shrine entrances to ward off evil spirits.

Ganesha (Sanskrit): The elephant god and son of Shiva.

Garuda (Sanskrit): a class of deities appearing in the shape of birds of prey, one of which is Vishnu's 'vehicle'. Very common in Khmer iconography, often shown with the *naga*, its mythological enemy.

guru (Sanskrit): '(spiritual) master'.

Hanuman (Sanskrit): monkey general and ally of Rama in the *Ramayana*.

Harihara (Sanskrit): a figure combining the gods Shiva (on the right side) and Vishnu (on the left).

Harivarman (Sanskrit): 'the (King) protected by the wild beast (Hari, a name of Vishnu).

Hiranyakasipu (Sanskrit): demon killed by Vishnu in his *avatar* as *narasimha*.

Indra (Sanskrit): 'king', especially of the gods. Adopted as a prefix by a number of Khmer kings, e.g. Indravarman, and Mahendravarman (protected by the great Indra). Also the tutelary deity of the East quarter.

Jayavarman (Sanskrit): 'the (King) protected by victory'.

Kailasa, Mount (Sanskrit): abode of Shiva.

kala (Sanskrit): demon commanded to devour itself. Commonly sculpted over temple entrances as guardian.

Karma (Sanskrit): actions or deeds; often provoking suffering in subsequent existences (the first of Buddha's Four Truths).

khleang (Khmer): 'the royal treasure'.

kompong (Khmer, from Malay *kampong*): village by the shore. Used in many temple and place-names in Cambodia, e.g. Kompong Svay,' the village of the mango fruit'.

Krishna (Sanskrit): eighth *avatar* of Vishnu, whose exploits in the *Mahabharata* are frequently portrayed in Khmer relief sculptures.

Kurma (Sanskrit): One of the *avatar* of Vishnu, who supports Mount Mandara in the Churning of the Sea of Milk.

Lakshmana (Sanskrit): Brother of Rama.

Lakshmi (Sanskrit): Vishnu's consort.

laterite: red, porous, iron-bearing rock commonly found in South-East Asia; easy to quarry and clay-like when wet, but extremely hard when dried.

linga (Sanskrit): 'phallus'; the symbol of Shiva, both as the reproductive organ and as pillar.

Lokeshvara (Sanskrit): Another name for *Avalokiteshvara*, the 'Compassionate *Bodhisattva*', who is the Mahayana Buddhist ideal.

Mahabharata (Sanskrit): 'the great (war) of the Bharata'; Indian epic poem.

Mahayana (Sanskrit): the 'great vehicle' school of Buddhism, founded in the first century AD, or earlier. Jayavarman VII is the Khmer king most associated with its implementation.

makara (Sanskrit): a mythical sea monster with an elephant's trunk, frequently found on Khmer lintels.

meru (Sanskrit): the mountain at the centre of the Universe. The symbolic centre of Khmer kingdoms and state temples, and the funeral pyre at cremations (Khmer men).

naga (Sanskrit): the mythical serpent-guardian of the riches of the earth, frequently represented in Khmer art.

Nandi (Sanskrit): sacred bull, the mount or vehicle of Shiva.

narasimha (Sanskrit): the *avatar* of Vishnu as part-man, part-lion.

phnom (Khmer): hill, mountain.

Prajñaparamita (Sanskrit): female form of the *Bodhisattva Lokeshvara*.

prasat (Khmer, from Sanskrit *prasada*) : shrine, sanctuary tower.

preah (Khmer): as a prefix to temple or personal names: 'holy, sacred'; also the modern Khmer word for Buddha. E.g. Preah Khan, 'the (temple of the) sacred sword'.

Rama (Sanskrit): Vishnu's seventh *avatar*, hero of the Indian epic poem *Ramayana* ('the march of Rama') scenes from which are depicted in relief friezes on temples throughout South-East Asia.

Ramayana (Sanskrit): Major Hindu Romantic epic tracing the efforts of Rama to recover his wife Sita, kidnapped by the demon Ravana.

Ravana (Sanskrit): The multi-headed and multi-armed demon king of Lanka and villain of the *Ramayana*.

saka (Sanskrit): the name of an era in Hindu chronology used in Khmer inscriptions, beginning in AD 78.

sampot (Khmer): a length of cloth acting as a skirt for the lower body, and tied at the waist.

shastra (Sanskrit): 'treatise' in the general sense: prefixed variously to indicate e.g. a treatise on Law (Dharmashastra).

Shiva (Sanskrit): the supreme god (Mahadeva) of Hinduism, to whom the majority of Angkorean temples were dedicated.

simha (Sanskrit): lion.

Sita (Sanskrit): Rama's wife.

stupa (Sanskrit): Buddhist dome-shaped monument enclosing relics.

Sugriva (Sanskrit): monkey king and ally of Rama.

Surya (Sanskrit): God of the Sun and one of the three principal gods in the Rig Veda.

Ta (Khmer): 'ancestor'. Ta Prohm is ' (the temple of) the ancestor Brahma'.

Theravada (Pali): the 'Doctrine of the Elders' and the branch of Buddhism practised in Sri Lanka and South-East Asia. Also known as *Hinayana*, the ancient 'little vehicle' sect of Buddhism.

thom (Khmer): 'large, great'. Angkor Thom is 'the great capital'.

Udayadityavarman (Sanskrit): 'the (King) protected by the rising sun'.

Uma (Sanskrit): Shiva's consort. Also known as Parvati, Gauri and, in her terrible aspect, as Durga.

Valin (Sanskrit): king of the monkeys, brother of Sugriva and wife of Tara.

Varuna (Sanskrit): God of the Waters and Guardian of the West.

Vasuki (Sanskrit): the giant *naga* king used in the 'Churning of the Sea of Milk'.

Vibhishana (Sanskrit): Ravana's brother who joins forces with Rama.

Vishnu (Sanskrit): a member of the Hindu trinity, along with Brahma and Shiva, best known in his role as preserver of the Universe, through his ten *avatar* (see *Krishna* and *Rama,* above). The ninth of these is the Buddha. The greatest Khmer temple, Angkor Wat, is dedicated to him.

Wat (Khmer): Buddhist monastery, or pagoda.

yaksha (Sanskrit): general term for demon.

Yama (Sanskrit): God of Death and Judgement; guardian of the South.

Yashovarman (Sanskrit): 'the (King) protected by Renown'.

yoni (Sanskrit): 'womb', the female component of the *linga-yoni* sculptures in Khmer art, where the male element symbolises the Hindu trinity.

BIBLIOGRAPHY

This select bibliography omits reference to the enormous number of articles on Angkor, especially those published in French in the Bulletin de l'Ecole francaise d'Extrême-Orient, although many of them are crucial for a full understanding of the subject. It concentrates instead on books, some of which are pioneering works, while others are included for the quality of their illustrations or because they are available in English or in English translation. Readers who wish to dig deeper should consult Boisselier: *Le Cambodge* (Paris, 1966) which includes a complete and exemplary bibliography up to the date of its publication.

Ang Choulean,
Les êtres surnaturels dans la réligion populaire khmère,
Paris,1986.

Boisselier, J.,
Le Cambodge,
Paris, 1966.

Boisselier, J.,
Trends in Khmer Art
(trans. Eilenberg),
New York, 1989.

Briggs, L. P.,
The Ancient Khmer Empire,
Philadelphia, 1951.

Chou Ta-Kuan (nowadays rendered as Zhou Daguan),
The Customs of Cambodia,
Bangkok, 1992.

Chandler, D. P.,
A History of Cambodia,
Boulder, 1992.

Chandler, D. P. & Mabbett, I.,
The Khmers,
Oxford (UK) and Cambridge (USA), 1995.

Cœdès, G.,
The Indianized States of Southeast Asia
(trans. Cowing),
Honolulu, 1968.

Cœdès, G.,
Angkor: An Introduction
(trans. Gardiner),
London, 1963.

Cœdès, G.,
The Making of South-East Asia (trans. Wright)
London, 1966.

Dagens, B.,
Angkor, heart of an Asian Empire,
London, 1995.

Dumarcy, J.,
Le Bayon. Histoire architecturale du temple,
Paris 1967

Dumarcy, J.,
Ta Kev. Etude architecturale du temple,
Paris, 1967.

Dumarcy, J.,
Phnom Bakheng. Etude architecturale du temple,
Paris, 1967.

Dupont, P.,
La statuaire pré angkorienne,
Ascona, 1955.

Freeman, M.,
A Guide to Khmer Temples in Thailand and Laos,
Bangkok 1996.

Giteau, M.,
Khmer sculpture and the Angkor civilisation,
London, 1965.

Glaize, M.,
Les Monuments du groupe d' Angkor,
Paris, 1993.

Gorer, G.,
Bali and Angkor,
Singapore, 1986.

Groslier, B-Ph., & Arthaud, J.,
Angkor, Art and Civilisation,
London, 1966

Groslier, B-Ph.,
Indochina (trans. Lawrence),
London, mid-1960s.

Jacques, C.,
Angkor,
Paris, 1990.

Jacques, C.,
Angkor, vision de palais divins,
Paris, 1997.

Jacques, C., Geoffroy-Schneiter, B. and Zephir, T.,
L' ABCdaire d'Angkor et l'art khmer,
Paris, 1997.

Jenner, P.,
A Chronological Inventory of the Inscriptions of Cambodia,
Honolulu, 1980.

Jessup, H., and Zephir, T. (eds),
Angkor et dix siècles d'art khmer (Exhibition catalogue),
Paris, 1997.

Kulke, H.,
The devaraja cult,
Ithaca, 1978.

Leclère, A.,
Cambodge: Fetes civiles et religieuses,
Paris, 1917.

Lewis, N.,
A Dragon Apparent: Travels in Cambodia, Laos and Vietnam,
London, 1982.

Macdonald, M.,
Angkor and the Khmers,
London, 1987.

Madsen, A.,
Silk Roads: The Asian Adventures of Clara and Andre Malraux,
London, 1990.

Mazzeo, D. & Antonini, C.S.,
Ancient Cambodia (trans. Mondadori),
London, 1978.

Moore, E. & Siribhaddra, S.,
Palaces of the Gods: Khmer Art and Architecture in Thailand,
Bangkok 1992.

Mouhot, H.,
Travels in the Central Parts of Indochina,
London, 1864, rep. Bangkok, 1986.

Quatritch-Wales, H. G.,
The Making of Greater India,
London, 1951.

Rawson, P.,
The Art of Southeast Asia, Cambodia, Vietnam, Thailand, Laos, Burma, Java, Bali,
London 1967.

Rooney, D.,
Angkor, an introduction to the Temples,
Hong Kong, 1994.

Roveda, V.,
Khmer Mythology
Bangkok and London, 1997.

Stern, P.,
Les monuments Khmers du style du Bayon et Jayavarman VII,
Paris 1965.

Tarling, N., (ed.)
The Cambridge History of Southeast Asia, Vol. 1: from early times to c. 1800,
Cambridge, (UK), 1992.

Thierry, S.,
Les Khmers,
Paris, 1996.

Thomson, J.,
The Straits of Malacca, Siam and Indochina: Travels and Adventures of a Nineteenth-century Photographer,
London 1875, rep. Singapore, 1993.

Vickery, M.,
Cambodia after Angkor: the chronicular evidence for the fourteenth to sixteenth centuries,
Michigan, 1977.

Walker, G. B.,
Angkor Empire,
Calcutta, 1955.
Wheatley, P.,
Nagara and Commandery,
Chicago, 1983.

Swann, W.,
Lost Cities of Asia, Ceylon, Burma, Cambodia,
London, 1966.

INDEX